BATTLE
OF THE
AGES

GUARDING AGAINST DECEPTIVE SPIRITS
AND THEIR DESTRUCTIVE INFLUENCES

DEREK PRINCE

W
WHITAKER
HOUSE

Publisher's Note:
This book was compiled from the extensive archive of Derek Prince's unpublished materials
and approved by the Derek Prince Ministries editorial team.

BATTLE OF THE AGES:
Guarding Against Deceptive Spirits and Their Destructive Influences

This book was previously published as *Protection from Deception*. It has been reedited, restructured, and significantly condensed.

Derek Prince Ministries
P.O. Box 19501
Charlotte, NC 28219-9501
www.derekprince.org

ISBN: 979-8-88769-010-0
eBook ISBN: 979-8-88769-011-7
Printed in the United States of America
© 2008, 2023 by Derek Prince Ministries, International

Whitaker House
1030 Hunt Valley Circle
New Kensington, PA 15068
www.whitakerhouse.com

Library of Congress Control Number: 2023946190

1 2 3 4 5 6 7 8 9 10 11 ⦿ 30 29 28 27 26 25 24 23

CONTENTS

INTRODUCTION

In recent years, the church has witnessed a worldwide surge in signs and wonders—some biblical and helpful, others unbiblical and bizarre. Signs and wonders are not new phenomena; they are recorded in various Scripture passages and have been reported in different periods of church history. They extend beyond a specific church or denomination and have received attention from the religious and secular media alike. In the final analysis, the supernatural is the realm in which the *Battle of the Ages* takes place.

I harbor no personal prejudice or skepticism about unusual manifestations, primarily because I have experienced a number of such phenomena in my life, starting with my own conversion experience while I was serving with the British army in World War II. I will expound upon this in the first chapter.

TWO KEY QUESTIONS

One necessity for supernatural discernment is not to accept every unusual manifestation indiscriminately. Two questions should always qualify every such manifestation. First, is it an expression of the Holy Spirit of God, or of some other source? Second, is it in harmony with Scripture, or does it contradict the Word of God? As Paul attested in 2 Timothy 3:16, *"All Scripture is given by inspiration of God."* The Holy Spirit authored all of Scripture, and He never contradicts Himself. Therefore, every genuine manifestation of the Holy Spirit must concur with Scripture.

I once had close contact with a group claiming to experience supernatural manifestations. The group leaders were enthusiastic about the wonderful occurrences they experienced at their meetings. But when they invited us to join them, they instructed us not to test or examine them; we were simply to open up and receive them. This uncritical stance made me wary of this group's experience, because their method of acceptance without evaluation directly contradicts scriptural instruction. In 1 Thessalonians 5:21, Paul told believers to *"test all things; hold fast what is good."* Failure to test supernatural experiences is a failure to follow the mandates of Scripture.

WARNINGS TO HEED

Jesus provided distinct warnings against deception by false manifestations that will be ushered in at the end of the age. These admonitions are at the heart of the warfare we face in the *Battle of the Ages*. Four of these warnings are recorded within twenty-one verses in the book of Matthew. First, in Matthew 24:4, Jesus warned, *"Take heed that no one deceives you."* In verse 5, He foretold, *"For many will come in My name, saying, 'I am the Christ [Messiah],' and will deceive many."* In verse 11, He warned, *"Then many false prophets will rise up and deceive many."* Finally, in verse 24, He concluded, *"For false christs [messiahs] and false prophets will rise and show great signs and wonders to deceive, if possible, even the elect."*

These warnings are not to be taken lightly. Anyone who disregards them does so at the peril of his own soul. Deception—not sickness, poverty, or persecution—is the greatest single danger in the end of the age, and it is the final battlefield for us in the *Battle of the Ages.*

Anyone who denies his or her vulnerability to deception is already deceived, for Jesus has foretold it and He does not err. Our hearts are incapable of discerning truth on their own. Proverbs 28:26 teaches, *"He who trusts in his own heart is a fool."* We must not be fools by trusting our hearts. Whatever our hearts tell us is unreliable, as Jeremiah 17:9 attests: *"The heart is deceitful above all things, and desperately wicked; who can know it?"* In Hebrew, the word *deceitful* is active rather than passive. The heart is not deceived; rather, the heart is a deceiver, leading us astray.

TO WHAT END?

It is also important to realize that signs and wonders neither guarantee nor determine truth. Truth is established and unchanging; it is the Word of God. In John 17:17, Jesus prayed to the Father, *"Your word is truth."* The psalmist declared, *"Forever, O LORD, Your word is settled in heaven"* (Psalm 119:89). No event on earth, whether natural or supernatural, can change the slightest sign or letter in the Word of God.

True signs attest the truth; lying signs attest lies. Many Christians assume that every supernatural sign must be from God, forgetting that Satan, or the devil, is completely capable of performing supernatural signs and wonders. As Paul wrote in his second epistle to the Thessalonians,

DECEPTION—NOT SICKNESS,

POVERTY, OR PERSECUTION—IS

THE GREATEST SINGLE DANGER

IN THE END OF THE AGE.

The coming of the lawless one [the Antichrist] is according to the working of Satan, with all power, signs, and lying wonders, and with all unrighteous deception among those who perish, because they did not receive the love of the truth, that they might be saved. And for this reason God will send them strong delusion, that they should believe the lie, that they all may be condemned who did not believe the truth but had pleasure in unrighteousness.

(2 Thessalonians 2:9–12)

This passage proves that lying signs and wonders exist; a phenomenon is not true based solely on its classification as a supernatural manifestation. Recall that in Exodus, many of Moses's miracles before Pharaoh were matched by Pharaoh's magicians and sorcerers. (See Exodus 7:11–23.) Moses's staff-turned-serpent ultimately ate the serpents formed from the sorcerers' rods. But the fact remains that Satan can give people the power to perform certain miracles.

Those who accept Satan's lies do so *"because they did not receive the love of the truth….God will send them strong delusion"* (2 Thessalonians 2:10–11). This is among the Bible's most frightening statements. If God sends strong delusion, we are sure to be deceived. Condemnation comes to those who *"did not believe the truth but had pleasure in unrighteousness"* (verse 12).

THE ULTIMATE MEASURE

The only way to know whether a sign or wonder is true is to measure it with truth—with the Word of God. In John 8:32, Jesus said, *"You shall know the truth, and the truth shall make you free."* Scripture is the sole determinant of truth or falsehood. We are instructed to *"test all things; hold fast what is good"* (1 Thessalonians 5:21).

The book of Revelation promises a specific series of supernatural signs and wonders that will signify the end of the age. Our assignment in the *Battle of the Ages* is to practice discernment as we anticipate judgment day, guarding ourselves against the devil's tactics and holding fast to the true church, the bride of Christ.

HIS VICTORY, OUR VICTORY

As we await the day when our heavenly Bridegroom, Jesus Christ, will return to deliver us fully from this present evil age, we must be set apart from the world. When the Scriptures say *world*, they generally refer to the world system—the political and social order that rejects God, is ruled by Satan, and governs the minds and manners of people who have not been saved. Through Jesus's death and resurrection, God secured ultimate victory over the devil. Satan may rule this world, but his reign is fast approaching its end. Our deliverance—and God's glory—shall endure for all ages.

With this in mind, we are to share God's light and love with the world—not to be confused with falling in love with the world or seeking to receive its love. Focusing on our heavenly home, we must clothe ourselves with humility. We must put off all self-seeking efforts and motives. These only fuel our pride, a dangerous attitude that blinds us to Satan's deception and makes us vulnerable.

First and foremost, we must cling to the cross. It is the same instrument that deals Satan's death sentence and secures our salvation through Christ's victory—a victory that will be fully realized for us in the *Battle of the Ages*.

1

SIGNS, WONDERS, AND UNUSUAL MANIFESTATIONS

An unusual phenomenon that began occurring years ago in the church is no laughing matter to some. Believers of all ages and social backgrounds began experiencing prolonged outbursts of laughter. This spirit of hilarity seemed to be contagious, spreading through large groups. Some reported that this laughter stimulated their faith, drawing them closer to the Lord. Others, however, skeptically regarded this phenomenon as Satan's deception.

People would often ask me about the source of this laughter—could it possibly come from the Holy Spirit? I would tell them this was indeed possible. (I had to believe that, because laughter is how I came to Christ. Or should I say, laughter is how Christ came to me.)

MY JOYFUL CONVERSION

In the summer of 1941, I was stationed with a medical unit of the British army in a hotel on the North Bay of Scarborough in Yorkshire, England. The hotel had been gutted of its furniture, so we slept on straw mattresses on the floor. A nominal Anglican at the time, I was reading my Bible through from beginning to end, but not for devotional purposes. Rather, I regarded the Bible as a work of philosophy. As a professional philosopher, I deemed the work important to read as my academic duty. By this point, I had reached the book of Job.

In Scarborough, I interacted on several occasions with Pentecostal Christians. They were the first people ever to confront me with the necessity of receiving Christ as my personal Lord and Savior. Presented by the Pentecostals with the claims of Christ, I decided one night to pray until something happened. I did not know what to expect, but starting at eleven o'clock, I struggled for one hour to form a coherent prayer. Around midnight, I was distinctly aware of a divine presence with me and found myself repeating the words Jacob articulated to the Man with whom he wrestled at Peniel: *"I will not let You go unless You bless me!"* (Genesis 32:26).

With increasing emphasis, I repeated, "I will not let You go, I will not let You go," until I added, "Make me love You more and more…more and more and more…."

An invisible power came over me, and I found myself lying face-up on the floor with my arms in the air, repeating, "More and more and more…." Moments later, my words turned to deep sobs that rose up in my stomach and then shook my body before escaping through my lips. Half an hour later, an indescribable and involuntary change occurred:

my sobbing turned to laughter. Like the sobs, the laughter proceeded from my stomach. Gentle at first, it gradually grew louder, reverberating off the walls of the room.

The soldier who shared my room woke up to find me on my back, laughing uproariously with my arms in the air. He cast me several helpless glances and said, "I don't know what to do with you. I suppose it's no good pouring water over you." Within me, an inaudible response arose: "Even water would not put this out!" Not wanting to disturb my fellow soldier, I crawled to my mattress, pulled a blanket over my head, and laughed myself to sleep. I knew that the Holy Spirit was within me.

A CHANGED PERSON

When I awoke the next morning, I was a totally different person. No longer did vile language flow from my mouth. Prayer was effortless; it came as naturally to me as breathing. I could do nothing—not even drink a glass of water—without thanking God. At six o'clock that evening, I headed to the pub for my customary drink; however, it seemed as if my legs locked at the door, and I could not enter. I stopped trying to move my legs when I realized the pub's fare no longer tempted me.

I returned to my billet and opened my Bible, which had become a new book overnight. It seemed as if God and I were the only two people in the universe. God spoke directly to me through the Bible text. I opened to Psalm 126:1–2, which reads, *"When the LORD brought back the captivity of Zion, we were like those who dream. Then our mouth was filled with laughter."* "That's exactly what happened to me," I thought. "It wasn't I who was laughing. My mouth was being filled with laughter from some other source!" Upon further reflection, I realized that this strange, supernatural laughter expressed the same joy and excitement of God's people when He delivered them from captivity.

In Job, I came across another relevant passage: *"Behold, God will not cast away the blameless….He will yet fill your mouth with laughing, and your lips with rejoicing"* (Job 8:20–21). This laughter does not result from a person's own will; it comes from God Himself as a response to the assurance of His acceptance.

GOD'S LAUGHTER

In the book of Psalms, I made another discovery: God Himself laughs. His laughter is not, however, a reaction to something comical, but rather an expression of triumph over His enemies. When a wicked man plots against a righteous man, *"The LORD laughs at him, for He sees that his day is coming"* (Psalm 37:13).

When earthly rulers scorn God's government, *"He who sits in the heavens shall laugh; the LORD shall hold them in derision"* (Psalm 2:4). Regarding the evils of unregenerate men, the psalmist writes, *"But You, O LORD, shall laugh at them; You shall have all the nations in derision"* (Psalm 59:8). The righteous can join in God's jubilation: *"The righteous also shall see and fear, and shall laugh at him* [the wicked, evil man]*"* (Psalm 52:6).

In addition to explaining the source of my laughter, the Bible shed light on the identity of the Person from whom I was requesting blessing: Jesus of Nazareth, the same Man Jacob encountered at Peniel. Jacob met Him before His incarnation; I met Him after His resurrection. Both man and God, this Person could have been none other than Jesus of Nazareth.

About ten days after my first encounter with the Lord, I was lying on my mattress in the barrack when I started speaking an unfamiliar language that sounded like Chinese. I recalled what I had heard in church about speaking with other tongues. At first, I spoke with timidity. As I relaxed, the words came freely, with forcefulness. They did not originate in my mind or mouth, but in my stomach, like the sobs and laughter.

The next evening, I spoke again in an unknown language—this time, it was different from the previous instance. The words possessed a marked, poetic rhythm. After a brief silence, I spoke again—in English.

GOD HIMSELF LAUGHS. HIS
LAUGHTER IS NOT, HOWEVER,
A REACTION TO SOMETHING
COMICAL, BUT RATHER AN
EXPRESSION OF TRIUMPH OVER
HIS ENEMIES.

The words did not originate in my mind, however, and their rhythm seemed to mirror that of the previously uttered speech. I concluded that what I was speaking in English was an interpretive rendering of what I had spoken in an unknown tongue.

UNCONVENTIONAL, BUT NOT UNBIBLICAL

While my laughter was an unconventional spiritual experience, it was no less authentic. In Matthew 12:33, Jesus explained the test for spiritual experience: *"A tree is known by its fruit."* What was the fruit of my strange experience? A life converted from sin to righteousness; a life shifted from agnostic dabbling in the occult to an unshakable faith in Jesus Christ as revealed in Scripture; a life that has brought forth fruit in God's kingdom. Since this experience, I have had several additional instances of supernatural laughter. I have even seen God touch other believers in a similar way. Supernatural laughter cleanses and exhilarates, and it has even prompted miracles of physical healing and deliverance from emotional burdens such as depression.

A second example from my experiences with unusual manifestations occurred while I was a pastor in London. One evening, I was praying with some people from our fellowship on the top floor of a four-story building when the building suddenly shuddered and shook for thirty minutes—it shook with the power of God. At this time, a lame man was miraculously healed and threw away his crutches. It was at the very time that we began to praise God and the building started to shake.

A similar sign in the early church was recorded by Luke in Acts 4:31:

> *When they had prayed, the place where they were assembled together was shaken; and they were all filled with the Holy Spirit, and they spoke the word of God with boldness.*

SUPERNATURAL LAUGHTER
CLEANSES AND EXHILARATES,
AND IT HAS EVEN PROMPTED
MIRACLES OF PHYSICAL HEALING
AND DELIVERANCE FROM
EMOTIONAL BURDENS SUCH
AS DEPRESSION.

THE BIBLICAL RECORD

The simple fact that something is unconventional or unusual should not provoke automatic wariness, for it may indeed be from God. In the Old Testament, God's prophets did some unusual things. Isaiah had to walk barefoot and naked for three years. (See Isaiah 20:1–4.) Ezekiel was required to lie on his left side for three hundred and ninety days and on his right side for forty days; he had to prepare his food on a fire of cow dung. (See Ezekiel 4:4–15.)

In the gospels, Jesus Himself healed people in unconventional ways. He healed a deaf mute by spitting and touching the man's tongue. (See Mark 7:32–35.) He healed a blind man by making clay from His own spittle and smearing it on his eyes. (See John 9:6–7.) In the book of Acts, many features and events of the early church are unconventional compared to the church today.

HISTORIC EVIDENCE

Unusual manifestations have long characterized the ministries of well-known spiritual leaders, including John Wesley, George Whitefield, Jonathan Edwards, and Charles Finney. Their ministries differed from the current trend in unusual manifestations, however.

First, the principal activity of these men was preaching God's Word. It was not unusual for Finney to preach a two-hour message. Today, most sermons are significantly abridged to suit the short attention span of listeners.

Second, these men made a fervent call to repentance in which a penitent spirit preceded the change. The same should occur today. But people clamor for "a refreshing" without realizing the prerequisite of repentance, which Peter articulated in Acts 3:19: *"Repent therefore and be converted, that your sins may be blotted out, so that times of refreshing may come from the presence of the Lord."*

In the Christian church, supernatural activity should be regarded with neither blind faith nor cynical skepticism. We are instructed to *"test all things; hold fast what is good"* (1 Thessalonians 5:21). We must apply Scripture to test any sign, as Hebrews 5:14 indicates: *"But solid food is for the mature, who by constant use have trained themselves to distinguish good from evil"* (NIV). Discernment and a diet of solid spiritual food will enable us to assess the authenticity of signs we encounter.

FIVE MOVEMENTS THAT WENT ASTRAY

Some movements start with a genuine prompting of the Holy Spirit, but they veer off track, straying from the truths of Scripture and ignoring God's guidance. I would like to review five examples. Within the overarching charismatic movement are five specific movements with which I have had a personal association that raise questions about their legitimacy and authenticity.

THE LATTER RAIN

In the Canadian province of Saskatchewan shortly after World War II, an outpouring of the Holy Spirit came to be called the "Latter Rain." Many people emigrated from the United States to Saskatchewan, and the lasting effect of this movement was a restoration of the gifts of the Holy Spirit. About one decade later, from 1957 to 1962, I was a missionary with the Pentecostal Assemblies of Canada, and I inquired why the members of the Pentecostal Assemblies seldom—if ever—exercised spiritual gifts. They told me that "Latter Rain" had the spiritual gifts. In other words, because Latter Rain possessed the gifts and went astray, they did not want the gifts because they feared they might do the

IN THE CHRISTIAN CHURCH,
SUPERNATURAL ACTIVITY
SHOULD BE REGARDED WITH
NEITHER BLIND FAITH NOR
CYNICAL SKEPTICISM.

same. This notion is unfounded and the people showed signs of being deceived. In addition, the leaders became proud and self-assertive, falling into immorality.

THE MANIFEST SONS OF GOD

Another example is the Manifest Sons of God, a persuasive group of men who strongly believed the Scripture that all creation is waiting for the manifestation of the sons of God. (See Romans 8:19 KJV.) Their ministry was powerful, particularly in casting out demons. But they would engage in prolonged conversations with these demons, seeking revelation from them. Seeking revelation from demons is unscriptural, as was their theological conviction that some members of their group had already received their resurrection bodies. (See 2 Timothy 2:18.)

THE CHILDREN OF GOD

Next were the "Children of God," who changed their name to "The Family." Their female leader was powerful and captivating, but she manipulated the minds of young people, undermining relationships with their parents and families.

WILLIAM BRANHAM

William Branham had a remarkable ministry with incredible scope. He was a gentle, humble man with a legendary ministry of the word of knowledge. Once, at a meeting in Phoenix, Arizona, he chose a woman in the audience from his position on the platform and told her, "Now, you're not here for yourself. You're here for your grandson." Next, he said her name and street address in New York City—it was all accurate.

On several occasions, after exercising his gift, Branham collapsed and was carried offstage. Ern Baxter, the Bible teacher at Branham's evangelistic meetings and a colleague of mine, once told me in private that "Branham had two spirits; one was the Spirit of God, one was not." After Branham died in an automobile accident, his followers embalmed

THERE ARE SOME COMMON

THREADS RUNNING

THROUGH ALL FIVE OF THESE

MOVEMENTS. ONE IS PRIDE,

WHICH I CONSIDER THE MOST

DANGEROUS SIN.

his body and kept it unburied until Easter Sunday, many months later, when they thought he would be resurrected. He was not.

THE SHEPHERDING MOVEMENT (ALSO REFERRED TO AS "DISCIPLESHIP")

Lastly, the "Shepherding Movement" began with the genuine, supernatural intervention of God. During a convention, three fellow preachers—Bob Mumford, Charles Simpson, and Don Basham—and I discovered that the man who was leading the convention was a practicing homosexual. We met to pray about how to address the situation, and by the time our prayer was finished, we knew that God had joined the four of us together. Subsequently, we made a commitment to cover one another in prayer, to submit our personal lives to one another's scrutiny, and to confer together before making any major personal decisions.

Later, however, selfish ambition took control and inexperienced men were being put in positions of authority. In addition, our minds were not renewed, nor were we unified in purpose or aligned with God's purpose.

There are some common threads running through all five of these movements. One is pride, which I consider the most dangerous sin. Proverbs 16:18 wisely warns, *"Pride goes before destruction, and a haughty spirit before a fall."* The second common thread is a mixture of spirits—truth and error, the Holy Spirit and other spirits. These other spirits enter during a person's decline from earthly to soulish to demonic (see James 3:15), concepts we will discuss at length in later chapters.

3

TESTING MOVEMENTS WITHIN THE CHURCH

Every trend or movement in the church must be tested to determine whether it is from God. I have emphasized the biblical principle that *"a tree is known by its fruit"* (Matthew 12:33). I have witnessed people who were "drunk" or "intoxicated" in the Spirit, but I always look for the fruit. What comes from these experiences of intoxication and other unusual states?

In the New Testament church, supernatural signs were always designed to follow and affirm the preaching of God's Word. In Mark 16:17–18, Jesus told the disciples,

These signs will follow those who believe: in My name they will cast out demons; they will speak with new tongues; they will take up serpents; and if they drink anything deadly, it will by no means hurt them; they will lay hands on the sick, and they will recover.

THE TEST OF FRUIT

Movements from God bear fruit that identifies them as such. The following are five primary fruits by which we can authenticate present moves in the church.

1. THE FRUIT OF REPENTANCE

In the New Testament, God demands repentance more than He demands faith. John the Baptist prepared the way for Jesus by calling people to repent. (See Matthew 3:2.) Anyone he baptized was required to first bear the fruit of repentance (see verses 7–8). When Jesus came, the first recorded word He preached was *"Repent."* (See, for example, Mark 1:15.) He instructed the multitudes, *"Unless you repent you will all likewise perish"* (Luke 13:3).

After His resurrection, Jesus told the disciples that when they preached to the nations, they should teach that repentance precedes forgiveness of sins. (See Luke 24:47.) Paul's ministry reflected the same priority: speaking in Athens, he said, *"God…now commands all men everywhere to repent"* (Acts 17:30).

What constitutes true repentance? It is not an emotion but a decision of the will—a decision to turn away from sin and unrighteousness and to submit unreservedly to the lordship of Jesus Christ. Repentance is first among the six foundational doctrines listed in Hebrews 6:1–2.

Without true repentance, no one can build his life as a Christian on a solid foundation. I have counseled hundreds of Christians through various problems, and I have reached the conclusion that at least half of the problems come from the failure to truly repent.

WITHOUT TRUE REPENTANCE,
NO ONE CAN BUILD
HIS LIFE AS A CHRISTIAN ON
A SOLID FOUNDATION.

The church has an urgent need to place renewed emphasis on repentance and on the confession of sins. Years ago, I was invited to speak in Hull, a small city in England. A group of leaders representing about fifteen churches had been meeting together for years to wait on God. They invited me to speak to them. These meetings differed from most others I attended because of their unique atmosphere. I preached a straight message, the gist of which was, *"If you need to confess sins, you can confess them to God, but the Bible also says to confess your sins to one another, that you may be healed."* (See James 5:16.) Once I invited those present to come to the platform to confess their sins, they came streaming down one by one for about two hours. To me, this was significant. I saw it as the fruit that comes when we are waiting on God.

Sin that we do not confess becomes a formidable barrier to revival. Until we confess our sins, all the preaching and praise songs in the world will produce no effect. We often think, "I do not have any sins that I know of." But if we wait a little on the Lord, He will often reveal them to us.

I once read in the journals of John Wesley about a strong Methodist Society in Yorkshire made up of people who would meet weekly to confess their sins to one another. This is hardly the modern plan for starting a church. But James 5:16 instructs us, *"Confess your trespasses to one another, and pray for one another, that you may be healed."*

We have access to God through the cleansing blood of Jesus, but first we have to walk in the light—we must walk with one another in fellowship, confessing our sins. If we are out of fellowship, we are out of the light, because walking in the light entails fellowship. Jesus's blood cleanses not in the dark, but in the light; thus, fellowship and confession of sins are crucial to being cleansed by Christ's blood. (See 1 John 1:9.)

2. THE FRUIT OF RESPECT FOR SCRIPTURE

Jesus called Scripture *"the word of God"* (see, for example, Mark 7:13; Luke 8:11), and He set His seal upon it with five simple words:

"the Scripture cannot be broken" (John 10:35). If we believe in Jesus, we believe in the Bible. By the same token, if we do not believe the Bible, we do not believe Jesus, either. In Isaiah 66:2, the Lord says, *"These are the ones I look on with favor: those who are humble and contrite in spirit, and who tremble at My word"* (NIV). Here God combines repentance—a humble and contrite spirit—with a fearful respect for His Word.

Why should we tremble at God's Word? There are many reasons, but here—briefly—are two important ones. First, God's Word is the way through which God the Father and God the Son come and make their home with us. (See John 14:23.) Second, we will ultimately be judged by God's Word. (See John 12:48.)

From the beginning of creation, God has worked through two agents: His Word and His Spirit. The Spirit of God moved first; then, God's Word went forth (see Genesis 1:2–3). Creation was the result. God's Spirit and God's Word work together in harmony. God's Spirit acts according to God's Word, and Scripture—God's Word—is inspired by the Holy Spirit.

God never contradicts Himself. Thus, every spiritual manifestation must be tested according to Scripture. (See 2 Timothy 3:16; 1 Thessalonians 5:20–21.) Anything that does not correspond to Scripture must be rejected.

3. THE FRUIT OF EXALTING JESUS

In John 16:13–14, Jesus promised His disciples, *"When He, the Spirit of truth, has come, He will guide you into all truth....He will glorify Me."* This passage reveals two important facts about the ministry of the Holy Spirit. First, His supreme function is to glorify Jesus. Any authentic spiritual manifestation also glorifies Jesus, focusing our attention on Him alone.

When human personality takes the stage and assumes supremacy, the Holy Spirit starts to withdraw. Exalting human personalities instead of the Holy Spirit has often inhibited genuine moves of the Holy

Spirit. Churches sometimes err when they replace Christ, the church's true Head, with a pastor or parish leader.

Pastors are wonderful people, but they cannot take the place of Jesus. The chief function of pastors is not to solve your problems but to help you cultivate your relationship with Jesus, the Head. Some people mistakenly make pastors their go-to people, assuming they have all the right answers. Some pastors overstep their place and wrongly control their congregations. They may even claim to be necessary channels of communication with Christ.

Years ago, I knew a successful, godly pastor in Sweden who had built the largest Pentecostal church in Europe. From time to time, he would say to his congregation, "Please do not put me on a pedestal. For if you do, God will have to let me fall." Charismatic personalities who occupy a pedestal incur the jealousy of God, who says in Isaiah 48:11, *"I will not give My glory to another."*

It is true that we must have spiritual mentors. But, more important, you and I must also have a personal relationship with Christ—one that enables us to hear His voice, discern His guidance, and know what pleases and angers Him. We must be sensitive to our Head.

Second, John 16:13–14 highlights the Holy Spirit's identity by using the pronoun "He" rather than "it." Just as Jesus is a person, so too the Holy Spirit is a person who draws believers together around the person of Jesus. When people describe their spiritual life as experiencing "it," rather than using a personal pronoun for Jesus or the Holy Spirit, they miss the mark.

4. THE FRUIT OF LOVE FOR FELLOW CHRISTIANS

In John 13:35, Jesus told His followers, *"By this all will know that you are My disciples, if you have love for one another."* The apostle Paul echoed this truth in 1 Timothy 1:5: *"The goal of our instruction is love from a pure heart and a good conscience and a sincere faith"* (NASB).

EXALTING HUMAN

PERSONALITIES INSTEAD OF

THE HOLY SPIRIT HAS OFTEN

INHIBITED GENUINE MOVES OF

THE HOLY SPIRIT.

Any "religious" activity not characterized by love and community Paul dismissed as *"fruitless discussion"* (verse 6 NASB). In 1 Corinthians 13:2, Paul also pointed to the importance of love: *"If I have the gift of prophecy and can fathom all mysteries and all knowledge, and if I have a faith that can move mountains, but have not love, I am nothing"* (NIV). Each of us must ask: Has my faith made me a loving person?

The church must undergo a similar interrogation. When a move of the Holy Spirit occurs, we must ask: Does it produce Christians who sincerely love one another, regardless of denominational labels? Does the movement cause such love that unbelievers wonder in amazement at the community and compassion of Christians?

5. THE FRUIT OF LOVING CONCERN FOR THE UNREACHED

Jesus told His disciples in John 4:35, *"Lift up your eyes and look at the fields, for they are already white for harvest!"* If these words were true in Jesus's day, their truth is even more urgent today.

Based on my extensive travel and worldwide ministry, I have come to the conclusion that we are living in the harvest hour. Many Christians who could be working in the harvest fields of the world are instead entangled in the snare of materialistic self-centeredness. A genuine move of the Holy Spirit must release a multitude of new laborers into the harvest fields.

DOES THE CHURCH PASS THE TEST?

If a significant number of Christians in a given movement pass most or all of the five tests of fruit I just described, we can safely conclude that it is indeed a genuine move of God. This does not mean, however, that everyone or everything in the move is without blemish or flaw. None of God's people is faultless. But God is amazing in what He accomplishes with weak and fallible people when they surrender to Him.

4

THE IDENTITY OF
THE HOLY SPIRIT

We need to be able to recognize the Holy Spirit. Then we will know when He is moving in the church—and when He is absent. The Bible introduces the triune Godhead in Genesis 1:1–2: *"In the beginning God created the heavens and the earth. The earth was without form, and void; and darkness was on the face of the deep. And the Spirit of God was hovering over the face of the waters."* We are first introduced not to the Father or to the Son, but to the Holy Spirit, who was *"hovering over the face of the waters."* The Holy Spirit moved with creative power on behalf of the Godhead, and this creative role carried through the formation of the earth and everything in it.

Genesis 1:3 says, "God said, 'Let there be light'; and there was light." Psalm 33:6 tells us, "*By the word of the LORD the heavens were made, and all the host of them by the breath [Spirit] of His mouth.*" God's creative power was channeled through His word and His Spirit, which executed His pronouncement.

GOD'S UNIQUE MOTIVE

The Hebrew name for God in Genesis 1, *Elohim*, is plural. *Im* in Hebrew serves the same function as adding *s*, *es*, or *i* to the ends of words in English to make them plural. The verb for "*created,*" *bara*, is singular, presenting a significant paradox between a plural subject and singular verb.

God is one, and yet He is more than one; He is simultaneously plural and singular. This truth is immediately introduced to us by the first three words of the Bible (in the Hebrew text) and runs throughout the Scriptures, shedding light on God's triune identity.

It is significant that God's Holy Spirit is the first person of the Godhead we encounter in the Bible. I believe that when we develop a personal relationship with God, initial contact is made not by the Father or the Son, but by the Holy Spirit, who introduces us to the Son.

Reflecting on our experiences as Christians, many of us will recognize that before we came to know Jesus, another influence was at work in our lives. Our way of thinking and our desires started to shift. We may have grown disenchanted with the way things were. This was no one but the Spirit of God stirring our hearts and preparing us for God's Word, which brings light.

I BELIEVE THAT WHEN WE DEVELOP
A PERSONAL RELATIONSHIP WITH
GOD, INITIAL CONTACT IS MADE
NOT BY THE FATHER OR THE SON,
BUT BY THE HOLY SPIRIT, WHO
INTRODUCES US TO THE SON.

COOPERATION WITH THE FATHER AND THE SON

God's Holy Spirit has a special role in the process of redemption. In every stage, Father, Son, and Holy Spirit cooperate to perform crucial acts.

The process of redemption began with Jesus's incarnation, explained in Matthew 1:18: "*The birth of Jesus Christ was as follows: After His mother Mary was betrothed to Joseph, before they came together, she was found with child of the Holy Spirit.*" Luke 1:34–35 describes Mary's incredulity and the angel Gabriel's response:

> *Then Mary said to the angel, "How can this be, since I do not know a man?" And the angel answered and said to her, "The Holy Spirit will come upon you, and the power of the Highest will overshadow you; therefore, also, that Holy One who is to be born will be called the Son of God."*

The Holy Spirit actually formed the infant Jesus within Mary's womb.

The Holy Spirit also played a key role in Jesus's miracles and ministry on earth. At the house of Cornelius after Jesus's death and resurrection, Peter summarized His ministry in one verse: "*God anointed Jesus of Nazareth with the Holy Spirit and with power, who went about doing good and healing all who were oppressed by the devil, for God was with Him*" (Acts 10:38). The Father, Son, and Spirit work together to help humanity, to heal the sick, and to defeat the devil.

Regarding Jesus's death on the cross, Hebrews 9:14 says, "*Christ… through the eternal Spirit* [the Holy Spirit] *offered Himself without spot to God.*" Again, we see three persons working together: Christ the Son offered Himself through the Holy Spirit to the Father.

The same is true of the resurrection: Paul recorded in Romans 1:3–4 that Jesus "*was born of the seed of David according to the flesh, and declared to be the Son of God with power according to the Spirit of holiness,*

THE FATHER, SON, AND SPIRIT

WORK TOGETHER TO HELP

HUMANITY, TO HEAL THE SICK,

AND TO DEFEAT THE DEVIL.

by the resurrection from the dead." Thus, the power that raised Jesus from the dead was the Holy Spirit.

Acts 2 describes Pentecost, when the Holy Spirit descended upon the disciples and caused them to speak in tongues. Peter, addressing the crowd, preached a sermon centered on the life, ministry, death, and resurrection of Jesus. Acts 2:32–33 says,

> *This Jesus God has raised up, of which we are all witnesses. Therefore being exalted to the right hand of God, and having received from the Father the promise of the Holy Spirit, He poured out this which you now see and hear.*

At Pentecost, the Father fulfilled His promise through the Son to pour out the Spirit on the waiting disciples. Thus, Father, Son, and Holy Spirit work together for the good of humanity, effecting our redemption and salvation.

THE IMPACT OF THE SPIRIT

Psalm 14:1–3 depicts a man whose heart is devoid of the Holy Spirit:

> *The fool has said in his heart, "There is no God." They are corrupt, they have done abominable works, there is none who does good. The LORD looks down from heaven upon the children of men, to see if there are any who understand, who seek God. They have all turned aside, they have together become corrupt; there is none who does good, no, not one.*

When the Spirit of God is absent, man's heart neither seeks God nor knows it should. The Holy Spirit alone fills people with a longing for the truth. It is only by His grace that people turn from sin, humble themselves, seek God, and place their faith in Him.

The Holy Spirit alone can impart holiness, which is necessary in salvation. The work of the Holy Spirit does not stop there, though. In Ephesians 2:18, Paul explained that God indwells the church of Jesus

Christ, His people who have been redeemed: *"Through Him* [Jesus] *we...have access by one Spirit to the Father."*

We have access to the Father through Jesus the Son by the Spirit—neither by doctrine nor by eloquent words. These will ascend no higher than the church roof without help from the Holy Spirit. No one approaches God except through the Holy Spirit. All Christians need a relationship with Him, something many of them lamentably seem to lack.

THE HOLY SPIRIT IS A PERSON

We must understand that the Holy Spirit is as much a person as God the Father and God the Son. He is not a theological abstraction or a phrase to conclude the Apostles' Creed. He is a real person, and the course of our Christian walk will be charted much differently when we relate to Him as such.

When Jesus took leave of His disciples, He assured them, *"When He, the Spirit of truth, has come, He will guide you into all truth"* (John 16:13). The original text is in Greek. Greek is a language in which the words are divided into three genders—masculine, feminine, and neuter—the corresponding pronouns of which are *he, she,* and *it.* The Greek word for *"Spirit," pneuma,* is neuter, so it would normally assume the impersonal, gender-neutral pronoun, *it.* This verse, however, overrides grammatical convention and uses a personal, masculine pronoun, *"He."* Why? To emphasize that the Holy Spirit is a person to whom you and I must relate as such. We must not relate to Him as a set of rules or as simply a doctrinal concept.

OUR PERSONAL HELPER

The Holy Spirit's identity as a person received further reinforcement by Jesus when He said to the disciples after His resurrection, *"Nevertheless I tell you the truth. It is to your advantage that I go away; for if I do not go away, the Helper ["Comforter" KJV] will not come to you; but if I depart, I will send Him to you"* (John 16:7).

This passage describes an exchange of persons. Jesus said He would return to the Father in heaven; once there, He would send the Holy Spirit, or Comforter. Just as Jesus is a person, so too the Holy Spirit, who came to take Jesus's place on earth, is a person.

This exchange is to our advantage, for Jesus said we are better off with Him in heaven and with the Holy Spirit on earth. Many people like to imagine being on earth with Jesus, watching Him teach and perform miracles. As wonderful as this would be, the Bible reveals that we can know God more intimately and come closer to Jesus through the Holy Spirit than we could by Jesus's mere physical presence on earth.

We require an advocate—someone who pleads our case before God. The Holy Spirit is the best advocate, and God sent Him to plead our case and to protect us against the devil's snares. (See Romans 8:26–27.) The Holy Spirit has an exclusive role as God's personal representative on earth.

THE HOLY SPIRIT
IN THE CHURCH

In 2 Corinthians 3:17, Paul said, *"Now the Lord is the Spirit; and where the Spirit of the Lord is, there is liberty* [or freedom]." In the New Testament, *"Lord"* represents the sacred name of God, which is *"Jehovah"* or *"Yahweh"*; it indicates a divine person.

Paul said, *"the Lord is the Spirit."* God the Father is Lord, God the Son is Lord, and God the Spirit is also Lord. Jesus is Lord over the church, but the Holy Spirit is Lord *in* the church; Jesus's lordship over the church is effective only insofar as the Holy Spirit is Lord in the church. Should a church truly desire Jesus as Lord, the Holy Spirit must first be Lord within that church.

This requirement presents a problem to many contemporary Christian churches whose members confess Jesus as Lord but fail to make the Holy Spirit Lord in their lives and in their church meetings. They impose labels and use terms that do not authenticate the true Holy Spirit.

How does the Holy Spirit dwell within the church, the body of Christ? Paul identified two ways in his first epistle to the church at Corinth. In 1 Corinthians 3:16, he wrote, *"Do you not know that you are the temple of God and that the Spirit of God dwells in you?"* The "you" in this passage is plural in the original Greek; Paul was speaking to Christians collectively as a temple of the Holy Spirit.

He continued this idea in 1 Corinthians 6:19: *"Do you not know that your body is the temple of the Holy Spirit?"* Here, Paul addressed individual believers. Not only does the Holy Spirit dwell in the church—a collective group of believers—but He dwells within each individual believer. God wants to take up residence in each of us, inhabiting our physical bodies. What humility on the part of our almighty God, creator of the universe!

WHY WE NEED THE SPIRIT

What does the Holy Spirit accomplish as He indwells us? First, He is here to complete the ministry of Jesus. Although Jesus had completed the perfect sacrifice on the cross, when He left the earth, His task of training His disciples was far from complete.

Jesus had to leave them after three and a half years of companionship and instruction. But He did not abandon them. Instead, He sent the Holy Spirit to be with them forever: *"I will pray the Father, and He will give you another Helper, that He may abide with you forever"* (John 14:16). Jesus promised to send *"the Spirit of truth, whom the world cannot*

NOT ONLY DOES THE HOLY
SPIRIT DWELL IN THE
CHURCH—A COLLECTIVE
GROUP OF BELIEVERS—BUT
HE DWELLS WITHIN EACH
INDIVIDUAL BELIEVER.

receive, because it neither sees Him nor knows Him; but you know Him, for He dwells with you and will be in you. I will not leave you orphans; I will come to you" (verses 17–18).

If we attempt to live the Christian life without the Holy Spirit, we do so as orphans. Jesus provided the Holy Spirit to meet our needs, but we must welcome Him and acknowledge our dependency on Him.

Jesus again called the Holy Spirit a *"Helper"* in John 14:25–26:

> *These things I have spoken to you while being present with you. But the Helper, the Holy Spirit, whom the Father will send in My name, He will teach you all things, and bring to your remembrance all things that I said to you.*

This passage is important, for it attests that the New Testament depended not upon the apostles' memories or cleverness, but upon the Holy Spirit, who inspired their records.

Jesus never penned a word; He left to His apostles the task of recording His life and conveying His teachings in the Epistles. We can rely on the accuracy of their writings, not because they were infallible authors, but because they were authors inspired by the Holy Spirit who brought to mind Jesus's teachings.

The Holy Spirit completes our education as Christians. As Jesus said to the disciples in John 16:12–13,

> *I still have many things to say to you, but you cannot bear them now. However, when He, the Spirit of truth, has come, He will guide you into all truth; for He will not speak on His own authority, but whatever He hears He will speak; and He will tell you things to come.*

Their distress at His departure rendered them incapable of absorbing additional teaching at the time. So, further instruction by the Holy Spirit was necessary.

HOW THE HOLY SPIRIT HELPS US

The Holy Spirit ministers to us with guidance, leading us daily. He provides us revelation, sharing with us what is to come—things spoken in heaven and manifested on earth.

Revelation is especially important during these days of increasing violence. We live in a dangerous time. All kinds of evil forces and violent acts are spreading and growing. We cannot open a newspaper without reading of crimes committed, evils perpetrated. To our advantage, however, we have someone who warns us of things to come.

God warned Noah, who by faith built an ark well before the flooding even began, in order to save his household. Jesus said that as it was in the days of Noah, so it will be in the days when He returns. (See, for example, Matthew 24:37–51.) In Noah's day, the earth was filled with violence; the thoughts of every man's heart were evil. All flesh was corrupt and perverse, engaging in immoral acts. (See Genesis 6:5.)

Only Noah was righteous before God. Because God showed him what would happen, Noah knew of the impending flood and prepared accordingly. In order to survive and fulfill our tasks as Christians in today's world, we will require a supernatural warning from God.

DISTINGUISHING BETWEEN SPIRITS

How can we recognize the Holy Spirit? How can we distinguish the Holy Spirit from other spirits? There exists a counterfeit spirit—one example is the "holy spirit" propounded by adherents of the New Age movement.

The Holy Spirit has the distinct attribute of holiness, as indicated by His name. He is holy. In Hebrew, *Holy Spirit* is translated "the Spirit of Holiness." His other names—including the Spirit of Grace, the Spirit of Truth, and the Spirit of Power—are subsidiary to the title "Holy Spirit."

Nothing unholy proceeds from the Holy Spirit. The Scriptures speak of the beauty of holiness. (See, for example, Psalm 29:2; 96:9.) When it proceeds from the Holy Spirit, holiness gives a person an internal beauty that may or may not be mirrored externally. In 1 Peter 3:4, Peter spoke of *"the hidden person of the heart"* and *"the incorruptible beauty of a gentle and quiet spirit,"* which God values highly.

Anything ugly—in a spiritual sense—does not proceed from the Holy Spirit. Twelve key words associated with this type of ugliness should identify anything they describe as being unholy: degraded, degrading, flippant, indecent, insensitive, rude, self-assertive, self-exalting, sham, silly, stupid, vulgar. These words never apply to the Holy Spirit.

We can identify the Holy Spirit with three additional tests.

1. THE HOLY SPIRIT CANNOT BE MANIPULATED

First, people who use a spirit to manipulate or dominate others practice witchcraft, for no one wields control over God's Holy Spirit.

People have long misused gifts of the Holy Spirit, as indicated by Paul in 1 Corinthians 13:1: *"Though I speak with the tongues of men and of angels, but have not love, I have become sounding brass or a clanging cymbal."* In this case, the gift of speaking in tongues—when misused—makes an empty, discordant noise.

Other spiritual gifts, such as a word of knowledge or a gift of healing, may be misused when people use them to achieve a certain end (often personal gain) or to promote a movement that opposes the will of God. Thus the Holy Spirit and His gifts are separate entities.

A gift of the Holy Spirit may be misused, but the Holy Spirit cannot be manipulated. The Holy Spirit is God, and we must relate to Him as such.

2. THE HOLY SPIRIT IS A SERVANT

A second distinguishing feature of the Holy Spirit is His role as a servant of God the Father and God the Son. This reinforces the honorable nature of servitude, something resented and rejected by many people today who miss the importance of serving. The Holy Spirit's role as a servant directs His activities and attributes. In John 16:13–14, Jesus described the Holy Spirit's ministry and activity:

> When He, the Spirit of truth, has come, He will guide you into all truth; for He will not speak on His own authority, but whatever He hears He will speak; and He will tell you things to come. He will glorify Me, for He will take of what is Mine and declare it to you.

Thus, the Holy Spirit speaks no message of His own, but rather what He hears from the Father and the Son. His aim is to point to Jesus and to glorify Him. Any spirit that focuses on itself, rather than Jesus, is not the Holy Spirit.

3. THE HOLY SPIRIT GLORIFIES JESUS

A third attribute of the Holy Spirit has already been mentioned in our previous point, but it is worth noting here—Jesus's statement about the Holy Spirit in John 16:14: "*He* [the Holy Spirit] *will glorify Me.*" Everything the Holy Spirit does glorifies Jesus. This provides a foolproof test of whether something is of the Holy Spirit: Does it glorify Jesus?

The Holy Spirit will never glorify a human personality, a doctrine, a movement, a denomination...the list could go on and on. Nothing and no one other than Jesus receives His glory. If we desire the Holy Spirit in our lives and in our worship services, the best way to attract Him is by glorifying Jesus. When we lift up Jesus—praising Him, proclaiming His victory, declaring His righteousness—this aligns us with God's will and attracts His favor and blessing.

I recall a particular Sunday morning worship service in which the service flowed; you felt like you were on a cloud. I said to the worship leader, "That was a beautiful service this morning. Do you know why?"

Then I answered my own question: "Because Jesus was the theme all the way through, from beginning to end. That's what the Holy Spirit likes."

If we desire the Holy Spirit's anointing on our lives, in our services, and in our homes, we need to glorify Jesus—speaking about Him and worshipping Him. When we do, the Holy Spirit will gladly join the gathering.

THE DIVINE ADMINISTRATOR

Not only will the Holy Spirit glorify Jesus, but Jesus said the Holy Spirit also *"will take of what is Mine and declare it to you. All things that the Father has are Mine. Therefore I said that He will take of Mine and declare it to you"* (John 16:14–15). The Father has committed all He has to the Son, and everything shared by Father and Son—the sum of their wealth—is controlled by the Holy Spirit. He administers the wealth of the Godhead. To share in that wealth, we must befriend Him by glorifying Jesus.

In the British army, I was once in charge of distributing rations in a hospital. I was popular and had many friends. Why? Because people found that by being my friend, they could obtain a little extra tea or sugar—two valuable and rare items in those days. If we want God's best, we must be friends with the Holy Spirit. He will bestow generous portions of blessings on us.

THE BENEFITS OF BEFRIENDING THE HOLY SPIRIT

To summarize, the benefits of befriending the Holy Spirit stem from His assignments in the church. As we have seen, some of these are teacher, reminder, guide, revelator, and administrator of wealth.

WE MUST *"WALK IN NEWNESS OF LIFE,"* OR DEPEND COMPLETELY UPON THE HOLY SPIRIT FOR THIS NEW WALK AS CHRISTIANS, JUST AS JESUS DEPENDED COMPLETELY UPON THE HOLY SPIRIT FOR HIS RESURRECTION.

Another assignment is to empower the body of Christ. In Acts 1:8, Jesus said, *"You shall receive power when the Holy Spirit has come upon you; and you shall be witnesses to Me in Jerusalem, and in all Judea and Samaria, and to the end of the earth."* Even though the disciples were already saved and were following Jesus, they were still powerless to complete their commission single-handedly.

After Jesus's resurrection, the disciples spent every day praising God in the temple. This was wonderful, except that the rest of Jerusalem had no idea what was happening. When the Holy Spirit came, however, it took only a few hours for everyone in Jerusalem to know something was astir. When the Holy Spirit moves, He influences people and makes an impact. He stirs people up and renders apathy impossible.

We depend upon the Holy Spirit, just as Jesus Christ did before us. In Romans 6:4, Paul said, *"Therefore we were buried with Him [Jesus] through baptism into death, that just as Christ was raised from the dead by the glory of the Father, even so we also should walk in newness of life."*

The glory of the Father—the Spirit of God—raised Jesus Christ from the dead. Jesus did not raise Himself. Rather, He trusted the Father to raise Him by the Spirit. We must therefore *"walk in newness of life,"* or depend completely upon the Holy Spirit for this new walk as Christians, just as Jesus depended completely upon the Holy Spirit for His resurrection.

THE POWER OF THE SPIRIT

Our own strength and wisdom will fail; neither education nor financial resources will suffice. Only by the supernatural power of the Holy Spirit can we live the type of life God expects of us. Only by the supernatural power of the Holy Spirit may we accomplish God's purpose for our lives.

The word *supernatural* makes many people uneasy. But removing all references to the supernatural in the twenty-eight chapters of the book of Acts would obliterate the book altogether. In other words, the supernatural is not strictly something from the Old Testament. New Testament Christianity—which includes today and tomorrow—also involves the supernatural.

We have no hope of victory over sin without the supernatural power of the Holy Spirit. Friendship with Him helps us to cultivate true Christian character. We must speak of the Holy Spirit with respect and honor, and any blasphemy—defined as "to speak lightly or amiss of sacred things"—requires repentance. Let us make friends with the Holy Spirit today.

HUMAN PERSONALITY
AND THE HOLY SPIRIT

*N*ow may the God of peace Himself sanctify you completely; and may your whole spirit, soul, and body be preserved blameless at the coming of our Lord Jesus Christ" (1 Thessalonians 5:23). One great truth of this verse is that it contains the formula for the components of the human personality.

THE HUMAN PERSONALITY

Most of us would agree that spirit, soul, and body constitute the complete human personality. The first chapter of Genesis says that

God chose to make man in His own "*image*" and "*likeness*" (verse 26). Image refers to outward appearance; thus, something in man's outward appearance mirrors the outward appearance of God. Likeness refers to the internal structure of the triune Godhead: Father, Son, and Holy Spirit. Man's spirit, soul, and body correspond to the three components of the Trinity.

This internal structure of the human personality is traceable to God's creation of man. The human spirit proceeds from God's breath; He breathed into Adam to produce a spirit within him (see Genesis 2:7). Interestingly, in both Hebrew and Greek, the words for *spirit* and *breath* are the same. The body was clay infused with divine life to become Adam.

Proceeding from the union of spirit and body, the soul is perhaps the most difficult component to understand. It is the unique ego of each individual, the part that determines "I will" or "I won't."

Comprising will, emotions, and intellect, the soul produces statements of three corresponding types: "I want," "I feel," and "I think." These statements rule the life of natural, sinful man. When individuals surrender to these demands of their souls rather than being guided by God's Spirit, they separate themselves from God.

THE IMPLICATIONS OF SIN ON BODY, SOUL, AND SPIRIT

Let us consider what happened to Adam and Eve because of sin. First, the spirit died, for God said to Adam in Genesis 2:17, "*But of the tree of the knowledge of good and evil you shall not eat, for in the day that you eat of it you shall surely die.*" Even though Adam did not die physically for more than nine hundred years, he died spiritually the moment he disobeyed God by eating the fruit. All of Adam and Eve's offspring—all humans—are therefore rebellious by nature. When we repent, God does forgive our sins and renew our spirits.

A passage in Ephesians addresses these truths. In Ephesians 2:1–3, Paul wrote to believers who had been made alive in Christ:

SPIRITUALLY, WE ARE ALREADY
SEATED WITH CHRIST ON THE
THRONE. TO RECONCILE OUR
SOULS TO GOD, HOWEVER, WE
ARE RESPONSIBLE FOR TURNING
FROM OUR REBELLIOUS WAYS
THROUGH REPENTANCE.

You He made alive, who were dead in trespasses and sins, in which you once walked according to the course of this world, according to the prince of the power of the air, the spirit who now works in the sons of disobedience, among whom also we all once conducted ourselves in the lusts of our flesh, fulfilling the desires of the flesh and of the mind, and were by nature children of wrath, just as the others.

FROM REBELLION TO SALVATION

Salvation restores life to our spirits, as we read in Ephesians 2:4–6:

But God, who is rich in mercy, because of His great love with which He loved us, even when we were dead in trespasses, made us alive together with Christ (by grace you have been saved), and raised us up together, and made us sit together in the heavenly places in Christ Jesus.

God made us alive, resurrected us, and enthroned us—all in the past tense. These things have been accomplished. Spiritually, we are already seated with Christ on the throne. To reconcile our souls to God, however, we are responsible for turning from our rebellious ways through repentance. Many people who claim salvation have never renounced their rebellion.

Romans 5:1 teaches us, *"Therefore, having been justified by faith, we have peace with God through our Lord Jesus Christ."* We were at war with God, but our faith in Christ justifies us before Him, establishing peace between us. As we read in Romans 5:11, *"Not only that, but we also rejoice in God through our Lord Jesus Christ, through whom we have now received the reconciliation."*

While salvation cannot preserve our physical bodies, it does make them temples for the Holy Spirit to inhabit. We must treat them with reverence, as Paul exhorted in 1 Corinthians 6:19–20: *"Do you not know that your body is the temple of the Holy Spirit who is in you, whom you have from God, and you are not your own? For you were bought at a price; there-fore glorify God in your body."*

When we receive salvation, our spirits are made alive, our souls are reconciled to God, and our bodies are made temples for the Holy Spirit, so that we become eligible for the first resurrection—the bodily resurrection of those who belong to God in Christ.

FUNCTIONS OF SPIRIT, SOUL, AND BODY

SPIRIT

Our spirit is capable of communicating directly with God and worshipping Him, as attested by 1 Corinthians 6:17: *"He who is joined to the Lord is one spirit with Him."*

Neither soul nor body can unite with God; the spirit alone is capable of uniting with Him. And the spirit alone is capable of true worship. In John 4:23–24, Jesus said, *"But the hour is coming, and now is, when the true worshipers will worship the Father in spirit and truth; for the Father is seeking such to worship Him. God is Spirit, and those who worship Him must worship in spirit and truth."*

SOUL

The soul's function is to make decisions, and regeneration enables the soul to make right decisions. In Psalm 103:1, David wrote, *"Bless the* Lord, *O my soul."* In this verse, his spirit is telling his soul what to do. His spirit senses the need to bless the Lord, but he requires activation by his soul to execute this need.

It is often difficult to distinguish soul from spirit. The only effective dividing tool is described in Hebrews 4:12:

For the word of God is living and powerful, and sharper than any two-edged sword, piercing even to the division of soul and spirit, and of joints and marrow, and is a discerner of the thoughts and intents of the heart.

NEITHER SOUL NOR BODY CAN
UNITE WITH GOD;
THE SPIRIT ALONE IS CAPABLE
OF UNITING WITH HIM.
AND THE SPIRIT ALONE IS
CAPABLE OF TRUE WORSHIP.

The Word of God is the only instrument sharp enough to divide soul from spirit, and to discern their distinctions.

Two conditions to employ the Word of God in discernment are established in Hebrews 5:13–14, where the writer distinguishes between mature and immature Christians:

> *For everyone who partakes only of milk is unskilled in the word of righteousness, for he is a babe. But solid food belongs to those who are of full age, that is, those who by reason of use have their senses exercised to discern both good and evil.*

Discernment comes with practice and with prolonged study of the Word of God.

DISTINGUISHING SOUL FROM SPIRIT

The Greek word for spirit is *pneuma*, which means "breath," "wind," and "spirit." The corresponding adjective, *pneumatikos*, is translated as "spiritual."

The Greek word for *soul* is *psuche*; the corresponding adjective, *psuchikos*, means "natural," "sensual," "unspiritual," and "worldly minded." "Soulish" is a word that I created to encapsulate these meanings. Let's consider the differences between "spiritual" and "soulish" in relation to the body, as delineated in the New Testament.

BODY

Paul developed the concepts of spiritual and soulish bodies in his first epistle to the Corinthians. Referring to the resurrection, he wrote, *"It is sown a natural body [a soulish body], it is raised a spiritual body. There is a natural [soulish] body, and there is a spiritual body"* (1 Corinthians 15:44).

He continued in verse 46: *"However, the spiritual is not first, but the natural [soulish], and afterward the spiritual."* Our present bodies are soulish; our resurrection bodies will be spiritual.

I believe this transformation will mean that our spirits will direct our bodies, determining where to go, what to say, and what to do, no longer dependent upon the soul to carry out these decisions. We will be as the cherubim described in Ezekiel 1:12: *"Each one went straight forward; they went wherever the spirit wanted to go, and they did not turn when they went."* Verse 20 says, *"Wherever the spirit wanted to go, they went, because there the spirit went."*

7

PREVENTING DECEPTION

A passage from the book of James gives us a picture of the intervention of spirit, soul, and body. James 3:15 is pithy yet profound: *"This wisdom does not descend from above, but is earthly, sensual, demonic."* This passage marks the steps in the decline of wisdom, a decline that allows demons to infiltrate the work, people, and church of God.

Being earthly may seem innocent enough. But it takes little time for apathy to take root, dragging the individual down into the soulish realm, and perhaps further still into the realm of the demonic.

THREE STEPS OF DECLINE

1. EARTHLY

What does it mean to be earthly? From a Christian standpoint, earthly individuals focus on our earthly life and nothing more—nothing beyond. If an earthly individual is a Christian, he expects God to provide blessings applicable only to this lifetime: prosperity, healing, power, success, and other soulish pursuits.

To gain a better understanding of the earthly individual, it is useful to recognize individuals who were decidedly unearthly. One such example is Abraham:

> *By faith he dwelt in the land of promise as in a foreign country, dwelling in tents with Isaac and Jacob, the heirs with him of the same promise; for he waited for the city which has foundations, whose builder and maker is God.* (Hebrews 11:9–10)

Abraham accepted the temporality of earthly life, dwelling in a tent instead of building a residence in the Promised Land. By contrast, Lot, who separated from Abraham and turned toward the wicked town of Sodom, lived in a house and abandoned an eternal mind-set for a mundane one.

God expects us to adopt Abraham's mind-set. The world is not our home. When we forget that, we allow ourselves to become earthly in our focus.

A second example of an unearthly individual is Moses, described in Hebrews 11:27: "*By faith he forsook Egypt, not fearing the wrath of the king; for he endured as seeing Him who is invisible.*" Moses endured because he looked past the present hardships to a certainty of future fulfillment.

In 1 Corinthians 15:19, Paul wrote, "*If in this life only we have hope in Christ, we are of all men the most pitiable.*" If the purpose of our Christian faith is to receive blessings in this earthly life alone, we are to be pitied. Many have forgotten the fact that we are foreigners passing through this world, and consequently, their thoughts and ambitions lose proper focus. They become earthly.

2. SOULISH

Soulish is the level below earthly. What is the essence of the soul? As described previously, the soul is essentially the ego. Soulish people are egocentric, concerned exclusively with themselves.

While the spiritual person asks, "How can I glorify God?" the soulish person asks, "What's in it for me?" The contemporary church caters too often to this quest of personal gain instead of God's glory.

In 1 Corinthians 2:14–15, Paul wrote,

> But the natural [soulish] man does not receive the things of the Spirit of God, for they are foolishness to him; nor can he know them, because they are spiritually discerned. But he who is spiritual judges all things, yet he himself is rightly judged by no one.

The soulish man cannot discern spiritual truth because he must do so with the spirit; he is attuned solely to soulish appeals to his emotions. One can be motivated by soulishness to contribute a substantial tithe and/or offering to the church, but this improper motivation will render it ineffectual.

Soulish people worship God in order to have a good time. But the purpose of worship is not for us to have a good time. Rather, the purpose of worship is just what it says—worship! Proper worship praises God; it does not seek to elevate our emotions or to thrill our senses. In the process of worshipping God, our emotions may or may not be elevated or thrilled, but this should not be our primary focus.

Having been a preacher for many years, I have seen soulish appeals to emotion that move people to tears and make them excited—without changing them. One week later, they are usually the same. It is lamentable how many churches specialize in the realm of the soul rather than in the realm of the spirit.

THE PURPOSE OF WORSHIP IS
NOT FOR US TO HAVE A GOOD
TIME. RATHER, THE PURPOSE OF
WORSHIP IS JUST WHAT
IT SAYS—WORSHIP!

People in the soulish realm are carried away with little effort, setting themselves up for deception. This can be avoided only by distinguishing between the spiritual and the soulish realm.

3. DEMONIC

A step down from soulish is the demonic. The pattern of progression from earthly to soulish to demonic is perhaps best illustrated in the Old Testament by Aaron, a high priest of Israel who fashioned a golden idol. Exodus 32:1–6 describes his decline:

> *Now when the people saw that Moses delayed coming down from the mountain, the people gathered together to Aaron, and said to him, "Come, make us gods that shall go before us; for as for this Moses, the man who brought us up out of the land of Egypt, we do not know what has become of him." And Aaron said to them, "Break off the golden earrings which are in the ears of your wives, your sons, and your daughters, and bring them to me." So all the people broke off the golden earrings which were in their ears, and brought them to Aaron. And he received the gold from their hand, and he fashioned it with an engraving tool, and made a molded calf. Then they said, "This is your god, O Israel, that brought you out of the land of Egypt!" So when Aaron saw it, he built an altar before it. And Aaron made a proclamation and said, "Tomorrow is a feast to the Lord [Yahweh]." Then they rose early on the next day, offered burnt offerings, and brought peace offerings; and the people sat down to eat and drink, and rose up to play.*

There are several significant details in this passage to note. First, the people credited Moses for their deliverance—*"the man who brought us up out of the land of Egypt"*—instead of recognizing God's providence. Their focus on human leaders turned into idolatry.

The passage concludes with idolatry, too—*"the people...rose up to play."* Play is the essence of idolatry, and when our worship becomes play, we have slipped from the spiritual to the soulish, and—ultimately—to the demonic.

Much of what we call "worship" in our churches is not worship at all. It is self-centered, focusing on finding out how to obtain God's healing, blessings, and other provisions. Much music in today's church services appeals to the soul, stimulating it in the same way that secular music might.

RESTORING A SENSE OF AWE

In the New Testament, the book of Hebrews urges us to maintain the same awe of God that was inspired by Old Testament events, such as God's judgment on Sodom and Gomorrah. Hebrews 12:28–29 says,

> *Therefore, since we are receiving a kingdom which cannot be shaken, let us have grace, by which we may serve God acceptably with reverence and godly fear. For our God is a consuming fire.*

A New Testament example of God's holy judgment is His striking Ananias and Sapphira dead when they cheated with their offering. *"Great fear came upon all the church and upon all who heard these things"* (Acts 5:11).

How much awe do we find in today's church? In Britain one summer, I was talking with a minister friend who made the comment, "I meet people who talk about God as if He were someone they had met in the pub."

Many people view God as a casual friend or a close buddy. He does invite our fellowship and communion with Him, but we must never lose a sense of awe of God's holiness. Too often, the lack of awe gives way to unscriptural frivolity and flippancy. As Charles Finney once commented, "God never uses a jester to search consciences."

As the perversion of
something meant for good,
misplaced love can make
us candidates for
Satan's deception.

One ministry of the Holy Spirit is convicting us of sin. Where conviction is lacking, the work of the Holy Spirit is most likely lacking, as well.

AVOIDING SATAN'S TRAP

The condition of humanity is not about to improve. In 2 Timothy 3:2–4, Paul warned of what humans will be like at the close of this age. He listed eighteen moral blemishes that will be prevalent:

For men will be lovers of themselves, lovers of money, boasters, proud, blasphemers, disobedient to parents, unthankful, unholy, unloving, unforgiving, slanderers, without self-control, brutal, despisers of good, traitors, headstrong, haughty, lovers of pleasure rather than lovers of God....

We notice that this list is bookended by misplaced love—love of self, love of money, and love of pleasure. Soulishness, or the love of self, lets evil in. Verse 5 concludes, "*...having a form of godliness but denying its power. And from such people turn away!*" Despite their having a form of godliness—they were probably professing Christians—the people described here indulge in self-love and the vices this invites.

Satan takes great delight in those who love and exalt themselves, for he set the precedent for this attitude. (See Isaiah 14:12–15.) He leads people astray, encouraging them to love anything—money, pleasure, power, or themselves—more than they love God. As the perversion of something meant for good, misplaced love can make us candidates for Satan's deception. He takes what is good and pure, turning it into an instrument of our own deception and demise.

In the next chapter, we will learn more about Satan's tactics so we can recognize them and avoid succumbing to them.

8

SATAN'S EVIL AGENDA

Jesus will come to earth again for His bride, the church. But He is not the only one with plans for the end of this age. In the *Battle of the Ages*, Satan has always had schemes up his sleeve to disrupt God's purposes. To resist him, we must understand what they are. These objectives describe his goals for the end of the age.

Satan rules the unregenerate, but Paul wrote to converted Christians in Ephesians 2:1–3, reminding them of their liberation:

You He made alive, who were dead in trespasses and sins, in which you once walked according to the course of this world, according to

*the prince of the power of the air, the spirit who now works in the
sons of disobedience, among whom also we all once conducted ourselves in the lusts of our flesh, fulfilling the desires of the flesh and of
the mind, and were by nature children of wrath, just as the others.*

Satan rules the realm God originally committed to Adam's authority. When Adam sinned and fell, he surrendered his rule of the world,
turning it over to Satan. Satan's rule extends only to those disobedient
to God, however; when men and women return to God with true repentance, faith, and submission, they sever Satan's legal claim over them.

THE RESTRAINING FORCE

Moreover, Satan's control over mankind is not unlimited. While his
angel allies, who joined his rebellion, submit completely to his control,
humans' submission, expressed by disobedience to God, is only par-
tial. The Holy Spirit is the restraining influence who, by working in the
hearts of men and women to effect repentance and faith in Jesus Christ,
prevents Satan from taking complete control of humanity.

I believe the Holy Spirit operates through human channels to keep
Satan's power in check. An early example of such a channel was Noah
and his family, whom God preserved among all humanity from the
flood.

Satan has two primary objectives: to gain political control on earth
and to garner the worship of the world. As we approach the fulfillment
of God's objectives on earth, we also come closer to the fulfillment of
the goals of Satan. These goals will, however, be ultimately frustrated.

Throughout the centuries, Satan's plans have been frustrated by
the working of God's Spirit, who draws men and women back to God
through repentance and submission. When the Spirit succeeds, Satan's
dominion weakens. Left alone, the human race, which is naturally bent
on sin and rebellion, would pledge complete allegiance to Satan and turn
from God entirely. Thanks to the Holy Spirit, however, God's grace and

SATAN HAS TWO PRIMARY
OBJECTIVES: TO GAIN POLITICAL
CONTROL ON EARTH AND TO
GARNER THE WORSHIP
OF THE WORLD.

mercy move in the hearts of men and women, directing them to repent and seek God's countenance.

SATAN'S SUPERNATURAL SIGNS

As we established before, Satan has supernatural powers at his command. A conflict of supernatural powers will mark the end of this era in the *Battle of the Ages*: God versus Satan. In 2 Timothy 3:8–9, we read about Pharaoh's sorcerers who replicated the wonders performed by Moses:

> *Now as Jannes and Jambres* [magicians in Egypt in Moses's time] *resisted Moses, so do these also resist the truth: men of corrupt minds, disapproved concerning the faith, but they will progress no further, for their folly will be manifest to all, as theirs also was.*

At the end of the age, a clash will occur: the supernatural power of the Holy Spirit and the servants of God will battle against the supernatural power of Satan and his servants—magicians, wizards, enchanters, clairvoyants, mediums, and others who deal in the occult. Satan's servants will be put to shame, just as were the magicians in Egypt who mirrored only the first three of Moses's miracles.

Exodus 7:10 says, "*Moses and Aaron went in to Pharaoh, and they did so, just as the Lord commanded. And Aaron cast down his rod before Pharaoh and before his servants, and it became a serpent.*" Pharaoh summoned his sorcerers, who succeeded in turning their rods to serpents, but the finality is significant: Aaron's rod swallowed up the sorcerers' rods. (See verses 11–12.)

Pharaoh was not fazed, however, so the conflict continued in Exodus 7:19–22:

> *Then the* Lord *spoke to Moses, "Say to Aaron, 'Take your rod and stretch out your hand over the waters of Egypt, over their streams, over their rivers, over their ponds, and over all their pools of water,*

that they may become blood. And there shall be blood throughout all the land of Egypt, both in buckets of wood and pitchers of stone.'" And Moses and Aaron did so, just as the LORD *commanded. So he lifted up the rod and struck the waters that were in the river, in the sight of Pharaoh and in the sight of his servants. And all the waters that were in the river were turned to blood. The fish that were in the river died....Then the magicians of Egypt did so with their enchantments....*

Pharaoh's magicians turned water into blood, so Pharaoh questioned why he should heed Moses's message.

The pattern continued with frogs in Exodus 8:5–6:

The LORD *spoke to Moses, "Say to Aaron, 'Stretch out your hand with your rod over the streams, over the rivers, and over the ponds, and cause frogs to come up on the land of Egypt.'" So Aaron stretched out his hand over the waters of Egypt, and the frogs came up and covered the land of Egypt.*

The magicians replicated the process, and Pharaoh told Moses, in effect, "I do not need to listen to you, because my magicians did everything you did." Pharaoh's heart was then hardened, and he refused to honor Moses's request.

Moses finally made an impact with his subsequent sign in Exodus 8:16–19:

The LORD *said to Moses, "Say to Aaron, 'Stretch out your rod, and strike the dust of the land, so that it may become lice throughout all the land of Egypt.'" And they did so. For Aaron stretched out his hand with his rod and struck the dust of the earth, and it became lice on man and beast. All the dust of the land became lice throughout all the land of Egypt. Now the magicians so worked with their enchantments to bring forth lice, but they could not. So there were*

THE END OF THIS AGE WILL
LOOK EERILY FAMILIAR: MEN
WILL CHOOSE BETWEEN THE
TRUE CHRIST AND FALSE CHRIST.

lice on man and beast. Then the magicians said to Pharaoh, "This is the finger of God."

As in Moses's day, the final battle on earth will break out—not on the plane of human reasoning and argument, but on a supernatural plane.

WE MUST CHOOSE

Satan wants to distract man's attention and be worshipped. To accomplish these goals, he seeks out someone to grant him political control over the world. It was this aim that compelled him to tempt Jesus, offering power in exchange for Jesus's praise.

Satan sought to bestow power on Jesus so that those praising Jesus would, in turn, worship the source of His praiseworthiness, in this case Satan. (See Luke 4.) To this offer, Jesus responded, *"Get behind Me, Satan!"* (Luke 4:8).

Most people read this as an emphatic dismissal of Satan, but the language seems to say instead, "Follow behind Me." Jesus told Satan, "I will go first, and you may come afterward." Everywhere Christ is preached and proclaimed, the devil is permitted to follow, peddling an alternative: the false christ, or Antichrist.

This presents the human race with a choice: Christ or Antichrist. It also prefigures Pontius Pilate's presenting the crowd with the choice of whom to release from prison: *"Whom do you want me to release to you? Barabbas, or Jesus who is called Christ?"* (Matthew 27:17). They chose Barabbas, the criminal, bringing about the first manifestation in human history of the spirit of antichrist. Submitting to Satan's plan, the people rejected the true Christ and chose an evil, violent man.

The end of this age will look eerily familiar: men will choose between the true Christ and false christs. First, the true Christ will be preached in all nations, accompanied by signs and demonstrations of the Holy

Spirit. Next, Satan will follow, peddling the Antichrist. The decision will follow: Jesus or Barabbas? Jesus Christ or Satan?

9

SATAN'S STRATEGIES

Because Jesus refused to bargain with Satan in the wilderness, our adversary will select another man of remarkable ability and charismatic personality to win the world's favor. In the meantime, he employs two strategies: supernatural intervention by satanic spirits and a progressive corruption of human morals and ethics.

A decline in morality is already evident in the regimes of brutal rulers such as Adolf Hitler and Josef Stalin. Less obvious, but no less odious, is the use of supernatural intervention by satanic spirits.

Satan will also employ false prophets and put forth false christs to deceive and destroy followers of Christ.

INTERVENTION BY SATANIC SPIRITS

The Old Testament attests to this intervention by satanic spirits. Genesis 6:1–2 describes the time of Noah:

> *Now it came to pass, when men began to multiply on the face of the earth, and daughters were born to them, that the sons of God saw the daughters of men, that they were beautiful; and they took wives for themselves of all whom they chose.*

I believe *"sons of God"* refers to angels—angels who rebelled against God, breached the angelic realm, and cohabited with human women. Ancient myth and historical records from many cultures confirm this event.

Verse 4 continues,

> *There were giants [Hebrew, Nephilim, or "fallen ones"] on the earth in those days, and also afterward, when the sons of God came in to the daughters of men and they bore children to them. Those were the mighty men who were of old, men of renown.*

These *"men of renown"* are called "heroes" in Greek, and in Greek mythology, most heroes trace their origins to the union between a god and a human woman, such as Zeus and Leda. Intervention from Satan and his minions spawned a lasting legacy of sin and corruption in the human race. I have known at least three women who told me that demons sought to have sexual intercourse with them.

In 1 Peter 3:19–20, we learn that Jesus preached to the spirits in Hades: *"He went and preached to the spirits in prison, who formerly were disobedient, when once the Divine longsuffering waited in the days of Noah."* The book of Jude includes a similar entry:

The angels who did not keep their proper domain [i.e., did not stay on the heavenly plane], *but left their own abode, He has reserved in everlasting chains under darkness for the judgment of the great day; as Sodom and Gomorrah, and the cities around them in a similar manner to these, having given themselves over to sexual immorality and gone after strange flesh, are set forth as an example, suffering the vengeance of eternal fire.* (Jude 6–7)

Between His death and resurrection, Jesus descended into Hades, where God had imprisoned spirits for specific reasons. Greek mythology makes many references to a place called Tartarus, the same name used in the New Testament for the place where these imprisoned angels were cast. The standard Greek lexicon explains that Tartarus is a place of imprisonment, made for specific wrongdoing, located as far below Hades as Hades is below the earth's surface. In this respect, the Bible and Greek mythology are in accord.

CORRUPTION IN ETHICS AND MORALS

The supernatural intervention by satanic angels was accompanied by moral decline. Genesis 6:5 says, *"Then the LORD saw that the wickedness of man was great in the earth, and that every intent of the thoughts* ["every imagination" KJV] *of his heart was only evil continually."* Men's imaginations conjured vile notions.

Verse 11 continues, *"The earth also was corrupt before God, and the earth was filled with violence."* Violence and bloodshed were rife.

And verse 12 concludes, *"So God looked upon the earth, and indeed it was corrupt; for all flesh had corrupted their way on the earth."* Thus, prior to the flood, human degeneration was characterized chiefly by evil thoughts, violence, and sexual perversion.

The earliest event of God's judgment on the world, the flood, provides a glimpse of God's final judgment, too. Again, the Holy Spirit must work through a channel—in the case of the flood, He worked through Noah and his family.

In Genesis 7:1, God gave Noah the rationale for His choice: *"Come into the ark, you and all your household, because I have seen that you are righteous before Me in this generation."* Noah's righteousness sufficed for his family, too, a clear instance of what is declared in Acts 16:31: *"Believe on the Lord Jesus Christ, and you will be saved, you and your household."* When Noah and his family were safely withdrawn, God's Spirit withdrew from the rest of humanity, giving Satan free reign on earth for seven days, the time when Noah and his family were sealed inside the ark before the rain came. Judgment ensued, and in the final days a similar sequence will likely transpire. Jesus said in Luke 17:26, *"As it was in the days of Noah, so it will be also in the days of the Son of Man."*

ANOTHER WICKED RULER

Another Old Testament pattern that prefigures the end of this age occurred in the days of Ahab, a wicked ruler of the northern kingdom of Israel. His rule displayed both degeneration of human character and satanic supernatural intervention:

> *In the thirty-eighth year of Asa king of Judah, Ahab the son of Omri became king over Israel; and Ahab the son of Omri reigned over Israel in Samaria twenty-two years. Now Ahab the son of Omri did evil in the sight of the LORD, more than all who were before him. And it came to pass, as though it had been a trivial thing for him to walk in the sins of Jeroboam the son of Nebat, that he took as wife Jezebel the daughter of Ethbaal, king of the Sidonians; and he went and served Baal and worshipped him. Then he set up an altar for Baal in the temple of Baal, which he had built in Samaria. And Ahab made a wooden image. Ahab did more to provoke the LORD God of Israel to anger than all the kings of Israel who were before him.* (1 Kings 16:29–33)

THOSE WHO ARE NOT ROOTED
IN CHRIST AND ARE
IGNORANT OF THE POWER AND
TRUTH OF GOD WILL SUCCUMB
TO DECEPTION AND
ULTIMATE DESTRUCTION.

First Kings 21:25 describes Ahab's wickedness even more succinctly: *"But there was no one like Ahab who sold himself to do wickedness in the sight of the LORD, because Jezebel his wife stirred him up."* To whom did Ahab sell himself? To Satan, the author of wickedness—he made a bargain with the devil.

Ahab's wife, Jezebel, prefigures the harlot, or false church. She persecuted and put to death the prophets of the Lord and promoted instead false prophets. (See 1 Kings 18:4.) Her tactics represent what we can expect from the false church at the end of the age.

FALSE PROPHETS

Along with a false church, we expect false prophets and false christs to appear. Those who are not rooted in Christ and are ignorant of the power and truth of God will succumb to deception and ultimate destruction.

First Timothy 4:1 provides a clear warning: *"Now the Spirit expressly says that in latter times some will depart from the faith, giving heed to deceiving spirits and doctrines of demons."* Second Timothy 3:13 foretells, *"But evil men and impostors will grow worse and worse, deceiving and being deceived."*

Jeremiah 23:16–17 warns that false prophets speak of peace when true prophets would warn of destruction:

> *Thus says the LORD of hosts: "Do not listen to the words of the prophets who prophesy to you. They make you worthless; they speak a vision of their own heart, not from the mouth of the LORD. They continually say to those who despise Me, 'The LORD has said, "You shall have peace"'; and to everyone who walks according to the dictates of his own heart, they say, 'No evil shall come upon you.'"*

A prophet can speak comforting words. But if those who hear him are not walking according to the truth of God, these words do not apply. The prophet fosters false comfort. Jeremiah continues, *"For who has stood*

GOD JUDGES PROPHETS, PRIESTS,

PRINCES, AND PEOPLE,

BUT HE STARTS WITH THE

PROPHETS, WHO REPRESENT HIM

AND HIS WILL.

in the counsel of the LORD, *and has perceived and heard His word? Who has marked His word and heard it?"* (verse 18). A true prophet stands in the counsel of the Lord and turns people from evil ways.

False prophets cause many problems and lead astray people who look to the prophets as those who interpret God's will and God's ways. A false or fabricated interpretation leads astray those who subscribe to it. Ezekiel 22:23, 25–27 provides a vivid example:

> *The word of the* LORD *came to me, saying, "…The conspiracy of her prophets in her midst is like a roaring lion tearing the prey.…Her priests have violated My law and profaned My holy things; they have not distinguished between the holy and unholy, nor have they made known the difference between the unclean and the clean.… Her princes in her midst are like wolves tearing the prey, to shed blood, to destroy people, and to get dishonest gain."*

God judges prophets, priests, princes, and people, but He starts with the prophets, who represent Him and His will.

EXPECT AN INCREASE

In times of spiritual decline, false prophets multiply. In the time of Elijah, late in King Ahab's reign, there were four hundred and fifty prophets of Baal and four hundred prophets of Asherah, an immoral, pagan deity. That makes eight hundred and fifty false prophets, a stark contrast to the single true prophet, Elijah.

Also during Ahab's reign, Ahab used the testimony of four hundred other false prophets to convince Jehoshaphat, King of Judah, to go to war against Ramoth-Gilead. In this instance, too, there was but one true prophet, Micaiah. This period alone witnessed twelve hundred and fifty false prophets and only two true prophets.

Do you think this stark contrast is much different today? I believe the ratio of false prophets to true prophets has changed little since then.

10

CLEANSING THE LAND

In Ezekiel 22:23, God pronounced judgment on Israel: *"The word of the LORD came to me, saying, 'Son of man, say to her [the land of Israel]: "You are a land that is not cleansed or rained on in the day of indignation."'"*

When I was the principal of a college, a student named Wilson Mamboleo made a statement that has stuck with me: "The only thing that can cleanse a land is the rain of the Holy Spirit." Without the rain of the Holy Spirit, Israel was left unclean.

GOD'S DEALINGS

God goes on to describe how He will deal with four groups: prophets, priests, princes, and people. He deals with them in this order, starting with the prophet, who interprets God's will and God's ways to His people. Ezekiel 22:25–28 reads:

> *The conspiracy of her prophets in her midst is like a roaring lion....*
> *Her priests have violated My law and profaned My holy things; they*
> *have not distinguished between the holy and unholy, nor have they*
> *made known the difference between the unclean and the clean....Her*
> *princes in her midst are like wolves tearing the prey....Her prophets*
> *plastered them with untempered mortar, seeing false visions, and*
> *divining lies for them.*

God begins judgment with the church—with the prophets. False prophets abound, unfortunately. In Deuteronomy 13:1–4, Moses warns,

> *If there arises among you a prophet or a dreamer of dreams, and he*
> *gives you a sign or a wonder, and the sign or the wonder comes to*
> *pass, of which he spoke to you, saying, "Let us go after other gods"—*
> *which you have not known—"and let us serve them," you shall not*
> *listen to the words of that prophet or that dreamer of dreams, for the*
> *Lord your God is testing you to know whether you love the Lord*
> *your God with all your heart and with all your soul. You shall walk*
> *after the Lord your God and fear Him, and keep His command-*
> *ments and obey His voice; you shall serve Him and hold fast to Him.*

From the above passage, we see that false prophets give predictions that may even come to pass, but they are not from God because the predictions contradict the will of God as revealed in Scripture. Deuteronomy 18:17, 20–22 says,

> *And the Lord said to me: "...The prophet who presumes to speak*
> *a word in My name, which I have not commanded him to speak, or*
> *who speaks in the name of other gods, that prophet shall die." And*

WE MUST GUARD AGAINST BEING

DECEIVED BY FALSE PROPHETS,

WHO EITHER MAKE PREDICTIONS

THAT COME TRUE BUT

CONTRADICT THE SCRIPTURES

OR MAKE PREDICTIONS THAT DO

NOT COME TRUE, BECAUSE THEY

DO NOT COME FROM GOD.

if you say in your heart, "How shall we know the word which the
Lord has not spoken?"—when a prophet speaks in the name of the
Lord, if the thing does not happen or come to pass, that is the thing
which the Lord has not spoken; the prophet has spoken it presump-
tuously; you shall not be afraid of him.

We must guard against being deceived by false prophets, who either
make predictions that come true but contradict the Scriptures or make
predictions that do not come true, because they do not come from God.
It is unscriptural to permit someone to exercise the gift of prophecy
without checking what he prophesies. It must align with Scripture.

INFLUX OF THE OCCULT

An influx of the occult will characterize the end of the age.
Practitioners of magic, sorcery, and witchcraft will deceive themselves
and others, preparing the way for the Antichrist. Wizards, magicians,
clairvoyants, and other people who wield supernatural, satanic power
will grow worse and worse. We saw earlier that three of the miracles
Moses performed in God's name to make Pharaoh release the Israelites
from Egypt were matched by the wizardry of Pharaoh's magicians,
demonstrating Satan's power in the supernatural realm.

The wickedness of evildoers will increase, as will the goodness of the
righteous, as Revelation 22:10–12 instructs:

Do not seal the words of the prophecy of this book, for the time is at
hand. He who is unjust, let him be unjust still; he who is filthy, let
him be filthy still; he who is righteous, let him be righteous still; he
who is holy, let him be holy still.

Given such freedom, people will pursue their natural inclinations
to their logical end. To the wicked, the Lord says to live it up; you don't
have long. To the righteous, He says to pursue righteousness continually
without being complacent.

THE HOUSE OF GOD

"*The time has come for judgment to begin at the house of God; and if it begins with us first, what will be the end of those who do not obey the gospel of God?*" (1 Peter 4:17).

In Ezekiel 8:10–14, the prophet recorded what he witnessed in the inner court of the temple of Jehovah in Jerusalem:

> *I went in and saw, and there—every sort of creeping thing, abominable beasts, and all the idols of the house of Israel, portrayed all around on the walls. And there stood before them seventy men of the elders of the house of Israel, and in their midst stood Jaazaniah the son of Shaphan. Each man had a censer in his hand, and a thick cloud of incense went up. Then He said to me, "Son of man, have you seen what the elders of the house of Israel do in the dark, every man in the room of his idols? For they say, 'The* LORD *does not see us, the* LORD *has forsaken the land.'" And He said to me, "Turn again, and you will see greater abominations that they are doing." So He brought me to the door of the north gate of the* LORD's *house; and to my dismay, women were sitting there weeping for Tammuz.*

Inside God's temple, His people were worshipping hideous demonic figures. Women wept for Tammuz, a pagan fertility god who "died" at certain seasons of the year and was thought to be resurrected in the spring.

Ezekiel 8:16 continues,

> *He brought me into the inner court of the* LORD's *house; and there, at the door of the temple of the* LORD, *between the porch and the altar, were about twenty-five men with their backs toward the temple of the* LORD *and their faces toward the east, and they were worshipping the sun toward the east.*

For these abominable practices, God executes judgment on Jerusalem. He gave to those who mourned for the abominations special markings to protect them. Those without markings were destroyed. (See Ezekiel 9:4–6.)

Satan's allies are losers by default because Satan is himself a loser. His defeat is inevitable, so if we have aligned ourselves with him, we would be smart to switch sides while we can. He will not treat us fairly or compensate us for any efforts; once he is through with us, he will spurn us. Revelation 17:16 says,

> *The ten horns which you saw on the beast, these will hate the harlot, make her desolate and naked, eat her flesh and burn her with fire. For God has put it into their hearts to fulfill His purpose, to be of one mind, and to give their kingdom to the beast, until the words of God are fulfilled.*

Subjects of the Antichrist, the ten horns will ultimately destroy the harlot. Thus the false church will self-destruct, ruined by the same political power it manipulated to achieve its position.

THE CHURCH TODAY

This situation is not so foreign to the church today. In fact, I believe the same spiritual filth and abominations that infiltrated the temple in Ezekiel's day have also seeped into the professing Christian church of today.

Most noticeable of these abominations, especially among those in positions of authority, such as priests, bishops, and other clergymen, are feminism and homosexuality. Critics of the true church call it "patriarchal" and "hierarchical," attempting to overhaul its structure and practices.

Again, the person whom God will spare is he who cries and mourns for these abominations. Amos 6:3–6 illustrates this rather clearly:

> *Woe to you who put far off the day of doom, who cause the seat of violence to come near; who lie on beds of ivory, stretch out on your*

Satan's defeat is inevitable, so if we have aligned ourselves with him, we would be smart to switch sides while we can.

couches, eat lambs from the flock and calves from the midst of the stall; who sing idly to the sound of stringed instruments, and invent for yourselves musical instruments like David; who drink wine from bowls, and anoint yourselves with the best ointments, but are not grieved for the affliction of Joseph.

If we focus on enjoying ourselves rather than cultivating a concern for the sufferings of those around us, our spirits are far from that of Jesus.

For a more complete picture of the moral and ethical breakdown at the end of this age, we turn to 2 Timothy 3:1–5:

But know this, that in the last days perilous times will come: For men will be lovers of themselves, lovers of money, boasters, proud, blasphemers, disobedient to parents, unthankful, unholy, unloving, unforgiving, slanderers, without self-control, brutal, despisers of good, traitors, headstrong, haughty, lovers of pleasure rather than lovers of God, having a form of godliness but denying its power.

As the days draw to a close, we must be sure to disassociate ourselves from evil; from those who exhibit the aforementioned traits, 2 Timothy 3:5 tells us, *"Turn away!"*

We must decide with whom we will associate, for this will have great bearing on our eternal destiny. Satan plans to ensnare us. Let us resist his schemes and remain with those who follow the Lord.

11

WHAT MIXTURES CREATE

A mixture of good and evil yields two main results: confusion and division. Mixed messages contain grains of truth and falsehood, giving recipients two optional responses: they can focus on the good, or true, component and accept the bad along with it; or, they can focus on the bad, or false, component, rejecting the good along with it.

In either case, God's purposes are thwarted. In the church, confusion always yields division; fault lines form according to people's focus. The recent influx in signs and wonders indicates a mixture of spirits: the Holy Spirit and unholy spirits.

WARNINGS AGAINST MIXTURES

God warns against mixture in the Old Testament. Deuteronomy 22:9 instructs, *"You shall not sow your vineyard with different kinds of seed, lest the yield of the seed which you have sown and the fruit of your vineyard be defiled."* Furthermore, *"You shall not plow with an ox and a donkey together"* (verse 10), and *"You shall not wear a garment of different sorts, such as wool and linen mixed together"* (verse 11). God prohibits breeding mixed livestock, sowing with mixed seed, and wearing garments made of mixed material.

The principle conveyed by these prohibitions is that when you serve the Lord, you should not mix two different types of things. Sowing with mixed seed can represent a message comprised partly of truth, partly of error. Wearing a garment of mixed material is like living simultaneously in accord with Scripture and in accord with the pattern of this world. Allowing mixed livestock to breed can represent a Christian ministry group aligning itself with another group that is not Christian.

It is useful to note that when two different species are bred, their offspring is usually sterile. For example, mating a donkey with a horse yields a mule—an animal incapable of reproducing. Christian groups that join with "mates" of a different belief system—a different breed— often yield similarly sterile results.

King Saul presents a prime example of another biblical warning against mixtures of spirits. At one time, he prophesied in the Holy Spirit; at another time, he prophesied in a demonic spirit. Despite his forty-year reign, his victories as a military commander, and his other successes, mixture proved his death knell. Just before a battle, he consulted a witch; the next day, he committed suicide on the battlefield. King Saul's mixture of spirits and the dire results should serve to discourage us from mixing spirits in our lives.

We must ask ourselves, as individuals and as a church, whether we are sowing with mixed seed. Have I combined truth and falsehood? Am I wearing a garment of mixed materials—partly the righteousness of

WE MUST ASK OURSELVES, AS
INDIVIDUALS AND AS A CHURCH,
WHETHER WE ARE SOWING WITH
MIXED SEED. HAVE I COMBINED
TRUTH AND FALSEHOOD?

Jesus, partly my own fleshly nature? The blessing of God will not remain on that which is a mixture of purity and impurity.

FALSEHOOD CLOAKED IN TRUTH

Even accompanied by seeds of truth, evil is not to enter the church. We must not be passive or neutral regarding what we accept. Proverbs 8:13 instructs, "*The fear of the* LORD *is to hate evil.*" Compromising with evil is wrong, even sinful. The devil enters via evil with a goal "*to steal, and to kill, and to destroy*" (John 10:10). This goal applies to individuals and church congregations alike, and we must take an active stance of defense against the devil's schemes.

With regard to the working of God's Holy Spirit, many churches are fence-sitters—their congregations refuse to take a stance for or against, trying to reconcile God and the world, trying to keep friendly relations with both. When the Holy Spirit comes, He electrifies the fence—no more fence-sitting! We must choose one side or the other. Some churches resist the Holy Spirit to defend their neutrality, but Jesus says, in effect, "Whoever is not with Me is against Me." (See, for example, Matthew 12:30.)

AN INCREASE IN LAXITY

The trend today is toward permissiveness—and today's church is no exception. Possibilities seem limitless—you may find people dancing, clapping their hands, engaging in dramatic reenactments, or any previously unheard-of activities in church. These may be genuine efforts to praise God, but they may also be innovations to worship that promote distraction rather than devotion.

Increasing tolerance allows increasing freedoms; few specific restrictions deter evil. God, however, objects to the laissez-faire apathy of this age. As we saw in the last chapter, 2 Timothy 3:1–5 warns,

> *But know this, that in the last days perilous times will come: For men will be lovers of themselves, lovers of money, boasters, proud,*

blasphemers, disobedient to parents, unthankful, unholy, unloving, unforgiving, slanderers, without self-control, brutal, despisers of good, traitors, headstrong, haughty, lovers of pleasure rather than lovers of God, having a form of godliness but denying its power.

This forewarning of the degeneration of human character and conduct includes behaviors at which few people today even bat an eye. The above eighteen moral defects deal predominantly with misplaced love—love of self, love of money, and love of pleasure. Even people professing salvation—those *"having a form of godliness"*—are prone to exhibit these behaviors.

BLURRED BARRIERS AND BORDERS

The walls that have broken down in the church indicate fading lines of demarcation—boundaries that exist for a specific purpose of God. Based on the book of Genesis, there seem to be two boundary lines that God guards adamantly. The first of these is sexual intercourse between angels and humans, which I have already addressed in the preceding chapter. The second of these is the barrier between male and female, which nowadays has become blurred and obscured. Deuteronomy 22:5 says, *"A woman shall not wear anything that pertains to a man, nor shall a man put on a woman's garment, for all who do so are an abomination to the* Lord.*"*

The Hebrew word for *"abomination,"* *toebah*, is the strongest word for something God detests. While this does not mean that God has preferences about fashion and clothing styles, it does mean that there must be definitive distinctions between the appearance of men and women.

Language is becoming grievously generalized: instead of "man" or "woman," we say "person." Instead of "husband" or "wife," we say "spouse." These are two guidelines given by Microsoft in a software guide to writing, and they represent the ambiguity that God finds reprehensible.

AN EMPHASIS ON LOVE ABOVE OBEDIENCE

Some churches that move in unusual manifestations claim an emphasis on love. It is right to emphasize love, but not at the expense of obedience to the Lord. Any love that does not result in obedience is unscriptural. In John 14:15, Jesus instructed His disciples, *"If you love Me, keep My commandments."* First John 5:3 affirms this mandate: *"For this is the love of God, that we keep His commandments."*

Love for God is expressed in obedience. In a similar way, God's love for us relates to obedience: He chastens those He loves. As our Father, God disciplines us. In Revelation 3:19, Jesus stated, *"As many as I love, I rebuke and chasten. Therefore be zealous and repent."*

A British Bible teacher remarked that some Christians confuse "God is love" with its inverse, "Love is God." They assume that anything rooted in love cannot be wrong, forgetting that any love that separates people from God or produces disobedience to His Word is an illegitimate love.

PROPHECIES OF PARTIAL TRUTH

As we have seen, error can also enter the church through prophecy. Many people mistakenly think they must accept every prophecy, fearing the consequences of rejecting it. This contradicts New Testament teachings on prophecy, however. In 1 Corinthians 14:29, Paul said, *"Let two or three prophets speak, and let the others judge,"* and in 1 Thessalonians 5:19–21, he taught, *"Do not quench the Spirit. Do not despise prophecies. Test all things; hold fast what is good."*

Even though we are not to despise any manifestation of the Holy Spirit, we are indeed to test it, accepting only what is good and true. Prophets must allow others to judge them; if a prophet is not willing to be judged and tested, he should not prophesy. We must not believe prophets if they tell us, "If you judge my message, God will judge you." Rather, we must fear God's judgment if we fail to judge prophecies, for He tells us to do so. Prophets are not dictators!

SOME CHRISTIANS CONFUSE "GOD IS LOVE" WITH ITS INVERSE, "LOVE IS GOD." THEY FORGET THAT ANY LOVE THAT SEPARATES PEOPLE FROM GOD OR PRODUCES DISOBEDIENCE TO HIS WORD IS AN ILLEGITIMATE LOVE.

What standard are we to use when we judge prophecies? Read Isaiah 8:19–20:

> *When they say to you, "Seek those who are mediums and wizards, who whisper and mutter," should not a people seek their God? Should they seek the dead on behalf of the living? To the law and to the testimony! If they do not speak according to this word, it is because there is no light in them.*

The ultimate test of a prophet asks, "Does he speak according to the testimony of God's Word?" If not, there is no light in him.

Prophecy can be misleading. In Romans 12:6, Paul wrote, "*Having then gifts differing according to the grace that is given to us, let us use them: if prophecy, let us prophesy in proportion to our faith.*" In other words, prophets should not exceed the measure of their faith when they prophesy.

Prophesying can prove to be an exhilarating experience, and prophets can get carried away, even departing from what they actually receive from the Word of God and from the Holy Spirit.

For instance, someone may receive a true prophecy: "There will be a great revival." But he may grow so excited that he adds on, "And the revival will start in our church." The first part may be true, but the second part may be false (and vice versa). How can this happen? It occurs when a prophet goes beyond the proportion of faith that God has given him.

AN IMPROPER SOURCE

A prophecy may also be accurate but not have God as its source. Earlier we read an Old Testament warning about this possibility. Acts 16 gives an example of a prophecy or revelation that was not from God, albeit accurate. Paul and Silas had just arrived in the city of Philippi.

> *Now it happened, as we went to prayer, that a certain slave girl possessed with a spirit of divination met us, who brought her masters much profit by fortune-telling. This girl followed Paul and us, and*

cried out, saying, "These men are the servants of the Most High God, who proclaim to us the way of salvation." (Acts 16:16–17)

Every word this girl spoke was true. Furthermore, she was the first person in Philippi to correctly identify Paul and Silas and their role as Christ's servants. But it was not God's Spirit who was speaking through her; rather, it was a divining, fortune-telling spirit.

The passage continues, *"And this she did for many days. But Paul, greatly annoyed, turned and said to the spirit, 'I command you in the name of Jesus Christ to come out of her.' And he came out that very hour"* (verse 18). From that point on, the girl could no longer tell fortunes. It is amazing how many people practice fortune-telling—and how many times they tell the truth—but what they foresee is not from God. A lie is inevitably mixed in with the truth of their prophecies, but the truth acts as bait—if we bite it, we swallow the lie along with the truth.

I once heard about a young Christian woman who went to see a fortune-teller. The fortune-teller said to her, "You will soon be a widow. Your husband will be killed." Less than two years later, the young woman's husband was killed in a freak accident. Thereafter, the woman was racked with guilt, wondering, "Did I open the way for that to happen to my husband by going to the fortune-teller?"

Another example is more personal. At one point, I served on the pastoral staff of a church in the United States, and much of my time was spent in the ministry of deliverance. One woman approached me and said that she had been a spiritist, but she had repented and wanted deliverance. I had no foolproof evidence that she had repented, so I told her, "I am not convinced. Come back when you have really repented."

She left and returned one or two weeks later, saying, "I have repented." I was still unsure about the authenticity of her repentance, but I told her, "Okay, let us pray." We prayed, and it was quite a struggle. Afterward, I needed to rest. I reclined against the speakers' platform at the front of the church, and all of a sudden, the woman said, "I see you in a car and it is wrecked against a tree!"

I thank God that I was on my guard! I proclaimed, "You divining spirit, I am not going to be in any car that will be wrecked against any tree! I do not accept that!" I believe that had I accepted this woman's vision, it indeed would have happened. This was the destiny Satan had planned for me, and just as you receive God's destiny by being open to what He says, you can receive Satan's destiny by being open to what he says. I have never wrecked a car against a tree. Had I said, "That is terrible! I am going to wreck my car," things might have turned out differently. Do not accept Satan's destiny for your life, which he may try to convince you to accept by presenting you with things you know to be true.

FINAL JUDGMENT WILL SEPARATE MIXTURES

A parable about the kingdom of God presented in Matthew 13 speaks of the end of this age and the coming judgment on mixtures. A farmer planted seeds of good wheat in his field. At night, an enemy sowed tares—or weeds resembling wheat—among the wheat seed. As the crop grew, the farmer's field hands found tares growing amidst the wheat. (See Matthew 13:24–30.)

This field represents Christianity, or the kingdom of God, which includes people who bear appropriate fruit—like the good wheat—and others who bear no fruit—like the tares. The servants ask the farmer whether they should uproot the tares. *"But he [the farmer] said, 'No, lest while you gather up the tares you also uproot the wheat with them'"* (Matthew 13:29).

This response indicates that the outward distinctions between wheat and tares were negligible; crops producing fruit were often confused with those that produced no fruit whatsoever. The farmer's response mirrors Jesus's plan for believers and nonbelievers at the end of the age: *"Let both grow together until the harvest, and at the time of harvest I will say to the reapers, 'First gather together the tares and bind them in bundles to burn them, but gather the wheat into my barn'"* (verse 30).

A key difference between this fictional farm and the kingdom of God is the discernment of the reapers. While the field hands of the farmer found it difficult to distinguish wheat from tare, God's reapers are angels, who, like God, have no problem separating true believers from false believers.

Very often, Christians who are fed up with false believers attempt to oust them from the church. God tells us to have patience, however, and to abide the presence of tares until He uproots and discards them. Our primary responsibility is to make certain of our identity as wheat rather than as tares.

When I taught students in Africa, my aim was to counteract their objections to the gospel in order to win them to Christ. One principal objection they cited was the prevalence of hypocrites in the Christian church. Could I deny this observation? Of course not! In fact, it would be unscriptural to deny it, for the New Testament indicates that hypocrites will intermingle with true believers in the church. The presence of hypocrites affirms the truth of the New Testament; just make sure you are not among them.

STANDING IN THE GAP

In Ezekiel 22:29–31, the Lord catalogs the sins of the prophets, priests, princes, and people:

> *The people of the land have used oppressions, committed robbery, and mistreated the poor and needy; and they wrongfully oppress the stranger. So I sought for a man among them who would make a wall, and stand in the gap before Me on behalf of the land, that I should not destroy it; but I found no one. Therefore I have poured out My indignation on them; I have consumed them with the fire of My wrath.*

God sought a man to build a wall—this, I believe, constitutes restoration. He also sought a man to stand in the gap—to undertake intercession. A wall separates and divides, sequestering one place from another. Surrounding the contemporary church, most dividing walls have been demolished; we must restore them, and intercessors must stand in the gap.

Intercession is more than prayer; it is a permanent posture one assumes between God and the objects of His wrath. More than an occasional hour of prayer, intercession is a constant state. Abraham was a model intercessor. When the Lord planned to destroy the people of Sodom, Abraham supplicated on their behalf; he was rooted in intercessory prayer.

We must not compromise on biblical distinctions, especially because judgment will begin in the house of God. (See 1 Peter 4:17.) As God's representatives, we must portray Him faithfully and stand our ground on issues that are important to Him.

The antidote to mixture is truth—the pure, undiluted truth of God's Word. In a secular court of law, every witness must promise to speak "the truth, the whole truth, and nothing but the truth." How much more should we, as Christians, take a stand for the truth?

THE TRUE CHURCH IS THE BRIDE OF CHRIST

Mixtures of truth and falsehood, good and evil, have started to infiltrate the church. We are likely to be confused and deceived if we fail to discern between the two opposing churches on earth today: the true church and the false church.

In 2 Corinthians 11:2, Paul explained God's intentions regarding the true church: *"For I am jealous for you with godly jealousy. For I have betrothed you to one husband [the Lord Jesus], that I may present you as a chaste virgin to Christ."*

This is an amazing statement, considering the types of people who composed the congregation of the church at Corinth: prostitutes, homosexuals, lesbians, drunkards, fornicators, extortionists, and others. But Paul envisioned a church made presentable as a chaste virgin to the Lord Jesus Christ through the power of Jesus's blood and God's sanctifying work. Having founded the church at Corinth, Paul claimed responsibility for betrothing the church to Christ.

Thus the concept of the church's betrothal to Jesus Christ is an apt analogy. Anyone who has made a commitment to Christ is betrothed, but not yet married, to Jesus.

Revelation 19:7 provides a beautiful picture of the imminent wedding: "*The marriage of the Lamb has come, and His wife has made herself ready.*" All of heaven—the whole universe, in fact—eagerly awaits the marriage of the Lamb. God treats His bride—the true church—with love, blessings, and abundant provisions. He will share His throne with her for eternity. The concept of a betrothal between Christ and the church helps us to understand our proper relationship to Him and the church's proper attributes as His bride.

COMMITMENT

In Paul's day, betrothal was more binding than an engagement as we know it in contemporary culture. Today, a couple may break off their engagement without catastrophic consequences. In biblical culture, however, betrothal was a sacred and solemn commitment, almost as binding as marriage but lacking consummation.

Breaking the vows of betrothal was tantamount to breaking the vows of marriage; it constituted adultery. When a woman became betrothed to a man, the marriage ceremony followed soon thereafter, joining them legally as husband and wife. The true church is totally committed to Jesus, and He to her.

GOD TREATS HIS BRIDE—THE
TRUE CHURCH—WITH LOVE,
BLESSINGS, AND ABUNDANT
PROVISIONS. HE WILL
SHARE HIS THRONE WITH HER
FOR ETERNITY.

THE BESTOWAL OF GIFTS

Cleansing and purification prepare the church to wed her Bridegroom, Christ. Revelation 19:8 describes the church preparing for marriage: "*To her it was granted to be arrayed in fine linen, clean and bright, for the fine linen is the righteous acts of the saints.*" She will be adorned with jewels—the gifts of the Holy Spirit. Paul wrote in his first epistle to the Corinthians,

> *I thank my God always concerning you for the grace of God which was given to you by Christ Jesus, that you were enriched in every thing by Him in all utterance and all knowledge, even as the testimony of Christ was confirmed in you, so that you come short in no gift, eagerly waiting for the revelation of our Lord Jesus Christ, who will also confirm you to the end, that you may be blameless in the day of our Lord Jesus Christ.* (1 Corinthians 1:4–8)

When a man proposes marriage to a woman, he typically gives her a beautiful diamond ring. Can you imagine a woman agreeing to marriage but rejecting the ring? This response would render the prospect of marriage unlikely.

In the same way, the church that rejects Jesus's endowment of spiritual gifts will probably not become His bride. She needs to accept His gifts, being fully equipped and beautifully adorned for her wedding day. Isaiah 61:10 praises God for His adorning work:

> *I will greatly rejoice in the* LORD, *my soul shall be joyful in my God; for He has clothed me with the garments of salvation, He has covered me with the robe of righteousness, as a bridegroom decks himself with ornaments, and as a bride adorns herself with her jewels.*

Although some Christians have donned the garments of salvation, they have yet to put on the robe of righteousness. When Jesus saves us, He covers us with this very robe; if this prospect does not excite us as an engagement ring would a young bride, there may be something amiss.

THE CHURCH THAT REJECTS
JESUS'S ENDOWMENT OF
SPIRITUAL GIFTS WILL PROBABLY
NOT BECOME HIS BRIDE. SHE
NEEDS TO ACCEPT HIS GIFTS,
BEING FULLY EQUIPPED AND
BEAUTIFULLY ADORNED FOR HER
WEDDING DAY.

Again, the church prepares herself, *"arrayed in fine linen, clean and bright, for the fine linen is the righteous acts of the saints"* (Revelation 19:8). The wedding garment is woven of many linen threads that represent the righteous acts we have performed; if that is so, a great number of righteous acts will be necessary to make an entire gown. I sometimes wonder whether some of us will have enough material to weave such a garment. Some of us may be scantily clad; anticipating the wedding day makes us hasten to fashion a wedding gown that will cover us fully.

ANTICIPATION

Another characteristic of the church as bride should be an eager anticipation of her Bridegroom's arrival. Hebrews 9:28 says, *"Christ was offered once to bear the sins of many. To those who eagerly wait for Him He will appear a second time, apart from sin, for salvation."* The true church is excited about the return of Christ. He will appear to those who eagerly await Him. Can you imagine a bride twiddling her thumbs or yawning when she hears that her bridegroom is on his way?

A friend of mine who is a preacher once remarked that when Jesus returns, He will expect the church to say something more than simply, "Nice to have You back." Titus 2:12–13 tells us that we should *"live soberly, righteously, and godly in the present age, looking for the blessed hope and glorious appearing of our great God and Savior Jesus Christ."*

SUBMISSION

As Christians, we must commit fully to the true church, submitting to Christ, her Bridegroom. The relationship is modeled by Paul in Ephesians 5:22–23: *"Wives, submit to your own husbands, as to the Lord. For the husband is head of the wife, as also Christ is head of the church; and He is the Savior of the body."*

Christ is Head of the church, and His relationship to her is the same as a husband to his wife. As a faithful wife relates to her husband, so must the church relate to her husband, Jesus Christ. This relationship is characterized by love, honor, submission, faithfulness, and loving service. A wife submits to her husband; the church submits to Christ.

In Ephesians 5:25–27, Paul continued,

Husbands, love your wives, just as Christ also loved the church and gave Himself for her, that He might sanctify and cleanse her with the washing of water by the word, that He might present her to Himself a glorious church, not having spot or wrinkle or any such thing, but that she should be holy and without blemish.

When the church submits to God, it overflows with His glory and becomes beautiful. God will bring holiness to His church with the cleansing waters of His Word.

The Greek language has two terms for "word": *logos*, meaning the written word, and *rhema*, meaning a spoken word. Faith results from hearing the *rhema*, and so the preaching and teaching of God's Word will cleanse His church.

CHRIST IS THE HEAD OF THE CHURCH

In Ephesians 4:15–16, Paul used an anatomical analogy to describe our relationship to Christ:

Speaking the truth in love, [we] may grow up in all things into Him who is the head—Christ—from whom the whole body, joined and knit together by what every joint supplies, according to the effective working by which every part does its share, causes growth of the body for the edifying of itself in love.

The whole body depends on the head, by which it obtains instruction to grow, find nourishment, and function effectively. The same is true of the body of Christ, a fellowship that comprises all believers. An impaired relationship to the Head deprives the body of Christ of life-giving spiritual nourishment and direction. Deception impairs this relationship. Paul warned believers about this in Colossians 2:18–19:

Let no one cheat you of your reward, taking delight in false humility and worship of angels, intruding into those things which he has not seen, vainly puffed up by his fleshly mind, and not holding fast to the Head, from whom all the body, nourished and knit together by joints and ligaments, grows with the increase that is from God.

When we sever connection with the Head, we fall into error, deception, or false teaching that contradicts the truth of God. Believers can avoid these dangers by maintaining a right relationship to Jesus Christ, the Head. Let no one interfere with your personal connection to Him.

FOUR PRIMARY FUNCTIONS OF THE HEAD

Jesus Christ as our Head has four primary functions that can be understood in light of the functions of a head as it relates to the body.

1. First, a head receives input, both from the external environment via the five senses, and from internal systems, such as organs and cells that communicate with nerve receptors in the brain. God hears us—He knows our thoughts, our needs, and our longings.

2. Second, the head makes decisions, telling the body what to do. The head has sole decision-making capabilities. In John 15:16, Jesus told His apostles, *"You did not choose Me, but I chose you."* God chose to save you; the initiative to redeem the people of the world proceeds not from the world or its inhabitants, but from God. He chooses those of us who will bear enduring fruit, as Jesus elaborated in John 15:16: *"I...appointed you that you should go and bear fruit, and that your fruit should remain, that whatever you ask the Father in My name He may give you."*

3. Third, the head initiates action. The body's intentional muscular movement responds to stimuli sent by the brain. You may establish any number of religious programs in the church, but if God did not initiate them, they will bear no fruit whatsoever, much less lasting fruit.

4. Fourth, the head coordinates the activity of the body parts, which carry out the decisions it makes.

IMPLICATIONS IN THE CHRISTIAN LIFE

God's choice is crucial to our lives as Christians, and I believe God is involved in our lives to the degree that He has ordained what we are to pursue. Take marriage, for example. If you consider marrying, I advise you to marry the person God chooses. Do not decide for yourself.

I have been twice married; both wives have since gone home to be with the Lord. My first marriage lasted thirty years; my second, twenty years. Both marriages proved to be happy and successful, but only because God arranged them. I have never chosen a wife. God knew I was not intelligent enough to make the right choice, so He intervened and directed my path.

SERVING AND WAITING

In 1 Thessalonians 1:9–10, Paul wrote to some of the earliest Christians about the impact of the gospel in Thessalonica: "*They themselves declare concerning us what manner of entry we had to you, and how you turned to God from idols to serve the living and true God, and to wait for His Son from heaven.*" The Christians were responsible to both serve and wait.

These two functions define the totality of the Christian life. Serving is not all of it; serving should also be accompanied by waiting, or being still. (See Psalm 46:10.)

The Bible makes more than fifty references to the necessity of waiting on God or for God. The New International Version of the Bible provides a vivid translation of Isaiah 64:4: "*Since ancient times no one has heard, no ear has perceived, no eye has seen any God besides you, who acts on behalf of those who wait for him.*" God acts on behalf of those who wait on Him. Waiting is a mark of faith; it affirms your trust in God's providence. Waiting also acknowledges our dependence upon God.

I have a strong conviction that the church will not progress beyond its position today until it learns to wait on God. I believe Jesus will come back to a church that awaits Him, and that in God's providence, a period of time will come when we will cease to serve and simply will wait. The serving will be complete; all that will remain will be to wait.

13

THE FALSE CHURCH IS THE BRIDE OF THE ANTICHRIST

As I previously established, a false church will emerge from the true church, leading some believers astray as part of Satan's agenda for the end of the age. When did the church's cord first split into true and false strands? We must plumb the origins of Christianity—and the origins of human history—to discover the answer.

ORIGINS AND ATTRIBUTES OF THE FALSE CHURCH

The split between the false church and the true church actually began with Adam and Eve's two sons, Cain and Abel. Genesis 4:3–5 reads,

In the process of time it came to pass that Cain brought an offering of the fruit of the ground to the LORD. *Abel also brought of the first-born of his flock and of their fat. And the* LORD *respected Abel and his offering, but He did not respect Cain and his offering.*

Abel brought before God an acceptable sacrifice, and God was pleased; Cain brought an unacceptable sacrifice and resented God's disapproval. (See verses 5–7.) Let us consider the differences between these brothers and their sacrifices, for every individual is either a follower of Abel—the true church—or Cain—the false church.

First of all, Abel received a divine revelation, as indicated by Hebrews 11:4: "*By faith Abel offered to God a more excellent sacrifice than Cain.*" His faith evidences a divine revelation, for Romans 10:17 says faith comes by hearing the word of God. Somehow Abel knew that God commanded a living sacrifice be offered on the altar. By his sacrifice, Abel acknowledged the need for a sacrificial substitute to cleanse his sin.

Cain, on the other hand, rejected the requirements given through divine revelation and gave something other than a living sacrifice. Abel's sacrifice offered propitiation for the curse God put upon the ground in Genesis 3:17–18 after Adam and Eve disobeyed Him; Cain's sacrifice did nothing to revoke the curse, so his sacrifice was rejected. Abel's faith produced a martyr; Cain's lack of faith, a murderer. (See Genesis 4:8–12.) This contrast alone manifests the difference between them.

Abel's kind of faith produces the true church, which is the bride of Christ; Cain's lack of faith produces the false church, which is the prostitute and harlot church. Revelation 17:6 says, "*I saw the woman, drunk with the blood of the saints and with the blood of the martyrs of Jesus. And when I saw her, I marveled with great amazement.*"

Cain was a murderer; Abel, a martyr. The false church murders the righteous martyrs. These opposing attributes characterize the false church and the true church.

THE FALSE CHURCH IN THE OLD TESTAMENT

The false church is equated with Babylon of Old Testament history. This is indicated in Revelation 17:5: "*On her forehead a name was written: MYSTERY, BABYLON THE GREAT, THE MOTHER OF HARLOTS AND OF THE ABOMINATIONS OF THE EARTH.*" Babylon had several distinctive features that parallel features of the false church. First, Babylon persecuted the true people of God and destroyed the kingdom of Judah.

Second, it practiced idolatry and the occult. Isaiah 47:12–13 speaks of these practices:

Stand now with your enchantments and the multitude of your sorceries, in which you have labored from your youth....You are wearied in the multitude of your counsels; let now the astrologers, the stargazers, and the monthly prognosticators stand up and save you from what shall come upon you.

Jeremiah 50:38 also speaks of Babylon's idolatry: "*A drought is against her waters, and they will be dried up. For it is the land of carved images, and they are insane with their idols.*" An idol is anything that we put first in our lives besides God or consider more important than Him. Babylon was the capital city of idolatry and the occult in ancient times, and the false church is a spiritual Babylon.

Revelation 17:2 further describes the false church, "*with whom the kings of the earth committed fornication, and the inhabitants of the earth were made drunk with the wine of her fornication.*" Chapter 18 adds that "*the kings of the earth have committed fornication with her, and the merchants of the earth have become rich through the abundance of her luxury*" (verse 3). Fornication in this case means false religion, or idolatry. False teachings lead followers—the kings and wealthy merchants—into this fornication.

THE FALSE CHURCH AND POLITICAL POWER

Looking more closely at Cain's church—the harlot—one sees first that it exploits political power. From the time the Roman Emperor Constantine made Christianity the official religion of the empire in the fourth century, Christianity has been in decline. In the Middle Ages, the pope wielded two swords—one religious, another political—and the church experienced a backsliding.

The church is not called to run the political system. Rather, we are called to pray for our political leaders and to serve in the civic sphere when called upon by God.

Just as the true church is the bride of Christ, the false church is the bride of the Antichrist. The false church serves Satan, giving him all she has. He treats her as he does anyone who submits to him: he squeezes her like a lemon, extracting all the juice and discarding the peel.

THE FALSE CHURCH AND THE WEALTHY

As it seeks to gain political power and to manipulate world leaders, the false church aims its efforts primarily at the wealthy. This should arouse our suspicion, as should any group or movement aimed specifically at the affluent.

Jesus said the gospel is preached to the poor (see, for example, Matthew 11:5), and although this does not exclude the wealthy, where they are the sole audience, the message is probably not motivated by the Holy Spirit.

Wealth has long drawn people from true belief and into false religion or idolatry. Revelation 17:4 reads, "*The woman* [the false church] *was arrayed in purple and scarlet, and adorned with gold and precious stones and pearls, having in her hand a golden cup full of abominations and the filthiness of her fornication.*" With her "*golden cup*" of lavish wealth and ostentatious extravagance, the false church has seduced multitudes and has drawn them away from the truth.

THE CHURCH IS NOT CALLED
TO RUN THE POLITICAL SYSTEM.
RATHER, WE ARE CALLED TO
PRAY FOR OUR POLITICAL
LEADERS AND TO SERVE IN THE
CIVIC SPHERE WHEN CALLED
UPON BY GOD.

THE FALSE CHURCH AS AN UNFAITHFUL BRIDE

Again, the concept of betrothal provides a fitting illustration of the divergence of the false church from the true church. While the true church remains faithful to her vows of betrothal, the false church is unfaithful, breaking her vows and becoming a prostitute, an immoral harlot.

Paul explained how Christians come to break their commitment to Christ: *"But I fear, lest somehow, as the serpent deceived Eve by his craftiness, so your minds may be corrupted from the simplicity that is in Christ"* (2 Corinthians 11:3). Believers break off their betrothal when their minds are corrupted.

Corruption often comes when the gospel's simplicity is complicated and misapplied. The gospel message is simple. It contains historical facts stated succinctly in 1 Corinthians 15:3–4: *"Christ died for our sins according to the Scriptures, and that He was buried, and that He rose again the third day according to the Scriptures."*

The essential truths of the gospel are simple enough for a six-year-old to understand them; a six-year-old can often understand better than a twenty- or thirty-year-old can. Be wary when people invoke psychiatrists, philosophers, or scientists to endorse the Bible's validity; unlike other religions, such as Buddhism, Hinduism, and Islam, Christianity is tied to human history.

The false church is ushered in by false teachers, such as those who came to various churches after Paul had ministered there, and who added legal restrictions and complex elements to the gospel. Paul warned about these teachers in 2 Corinthians 11:4, saying,

> For if he who comes preaches another Jesus whom we have not preached, or if you receive a different spirit which you have not received, or a different gospel which you have not accepted; you may well put up with it!

The progression of these phrases—*"another Jesus," "a different spirit,"* and *"a different gospel"*—is significant. They center on Jesus, who said, *"I am...the truth"* (John 14:6). When you alter attributes of Jesus and present a historically inaccurate picture of Christ, you create a different spirit that results in another gospel.

Paul admonished the Galatians,

> *I marvel that you are turning away so soon from Him who called you in the grace of Christ, to a different gospel, which is not another; but there are some who trouble you and want to pervert the gospel of Christ. But even if we, or an angel from heaven, preach any other gospel to you than what we have preached to you, let him be accursed.* (Galatians 1:6–8)

The word *"accursed"* comes from a Greek word we also use in English, *anathema*. There is no stronger word to describe that which God completely condemns and rejects. If we receive a gospel other than the gospel of the New Testament, we are accursed unless we repent.

THE FALSE CHURCH EQUALS A FALSE VERSION OF JESUS

Three false versions of Jesus seem to prevail today. The first casts Him as a sort of oriental guru. The New Age movement, in particular, views Jesus in this way.

The second version of Jesus, promoted especially in South America, casts Him as a Marxist revolutionary. This view, known as Liberation Theology, teaches that Christians chiefly must feed the poor, eliminate the wealthy, demand social justice, and establish a new political order, forgetting that Jesus never made any of these things His chief priority.

Despite His great compassion for the poor and unfortunate, Jesus never sought to use force to establish a new social order. When He was arrested after Judas's betrayal, Jesus said, *"My kingdom is not of this world. If My kingdom were of this world, My servants would fight"* (John

18:36). Demanding social justice and political change in the name of Jesus contradicts scriptural teaching.

The third false version of Jesus is that of a universal Father Christmas: a jolly, benign fellow who walks around patting people on the head and saying, "There, there; never mind. It will all work out; don't worry." This false picture of Jesus is purveyed by liberal churches, where God's judgment of sin is scarcely mentioned.

RECOGNIZING THE FALSE CHURCH

First Timothy 4:1 warns of deception at the close of this age: *"Now the Spirit* [the Holy Spirit] *expressly says that in latter times some will depart from the faith, giving heed to deceiving spirits and doctrines of demons."* You cannot depart from the faith if you were never in the faith, so this passage is particularly sobering. It says that people who have believed the gospel and received Jesus Christ will go astray, following deceptive demons and false teaching.

False teachings will hinder the spread of the true gospel, and where the true gospel is preached, *"they will deliver you up to tribulation and kill you, and you will be hated by all nations for My name's sake. And then many will be offended, will betray one another, and will hate one another"* (Matthew 24:9–10). This effect has long been a reality. Jesus counseled, *"Then many false prophets will rise up and deceive many. And because lawlessness will abound, the love of many will grow cold. But he who endures to the end shall be saved"* (verses 11–13).

As Christians, we are promised persecution, betrayal, opposition, the rise of deception, and lawlessness. If you endure all this, you will be saved. This statement does not invalidate your salvation if you have secured it, but it means that to stay saved, you must endure.

What will indicate when this age is coming to an end? Matthew 24:14 provides the answer: *"This gospel of the kingdom will be preached in all the world as a witness to all the nations, and then the end will come."* In the face of mounting opposition and risk, the good news will spread

IN THE FACE OF MOUNTING
OPPOSITION AND RISK, THE
GOOD NEWS WILL SPREAD
THROUGHOUT THE WORLD AND
A SPECIAL BREED OF CHRISTIANS
WILL OUTLAST THE OPPOSITION.
THEY WILL RESIST THE
FALSE CHURCH.

throughout the world and a special breed of Christians will outlast the opposition. They will resist the false church.

COMING JUDGMENT ON THE FALSE CHURCH

Neither Babylon nor the false church will escape God's judgment. Revelation 18:8–10 foretells coming retribution:

> *Therefore her plagues will come in one day; death and mourning and famine. And she will be utterly burned with fire, for strong is the Lord God who judges her. The kings of the earth who committed fornication and lived luxuriously with her will weep and lament for her, when they see the smoke of her burning, standing at a distance for fear of her torment, saying, "Alas, alas, that great city Babylon, that mighty city! For in one hour your judgment has come."*

God will judge the false church in a swift act of finality and totality. Christians must discern the true church from the false church in order to separate themselves from the false church and the wrath she will incur, as Revelation 18:4 says: *"I heard another voice from heaven saying, 'Come out of her, my people, lest you share in her sins, and lest you receive of her plagues.'"* We must disassociate ourselves from this false religious system.

Second Timothy speaks in great detail about the necessity of separating ourselves from evildoers:

> *Nevertheless the solid foundation of God stands, having this seal: "The Lord knows those who are His," and, "Let everyone who names the name of Christ depart from iniquity." But in a great house there are not only vessels of gold and silver, but also of wood and clay, some for honor and some for dishonor.* (2 Timothy 2:19–20)

A "great house" such as the church contains vessels for honor and dishonor. Which type will we be? If we aspire to be vessels for honor, we must heed this passage:

Therefore if anyone cleanses himself from the latter [vessels for dishonor], he will be a vessel for honor, sanctified and useful for the Master, prepared for every good work. Flee also youthful lusts; but pursue righteousness, faith, love, peace with those who call on the Lord out of a pure heart. (verses 21–22)

If we desire to follow righteousness, faith, peace, and love, we must be with those who call on the Lord from a pure heart.

RECOGNIZING AND RESISTING
THE ANTICHRIST

The true church is the bride of the true Christ; the false church is wed to the false christ, or the Antichrist. The Old Testament word for Christ is "Messiah" (Daniel 9:25–26)—*Mashiach*, in Hebrew. Not only is there the true Messiah, Jesus Christ, but false messiahs exist as well.

A warning for believers appears in 1 John 2:18: *"Little children, it is the last hour* [the last period of this age]; *and as you have heard that the Antichrist is coming, even now many antichrists have come, by which we know that it is the last hour."* The word *"antichrist"* comprises two parts—*Christ*, which we just discussed, and *anti*, which in Greek means both "against" and "in place of." These meanings describe the aim of the Antichrist: to oppose the true Christ and to usurp His place. At the end of this age, many antichrists will appear and work to oppose Christ, seeking to replace Him.

Human rebellion will reach its peak before the Antichrist arrives; as Daniel 8:23 records, *"In the latter time of their kingdom, when the transgressors have reached their fullness, a king shall arise, having fierce features, who understands sinister schemes."* Most Bible commentators concur that the Antichrist is identical to this *"King,"* a king who will come once the rebels have reached the extreme.

FEATURES OF THE ANTICHRIST

The end of the age, therefore, will usher in the Antichrist—a specific, evil individual—as well as many antichrists, false spirits, and false prophets. False prophets speak with false spirits—spirits that deny Jesus's identity as Messiah. We are directed by 1 John 4:1 to test the spirits to know which prophecies and revelations to believe. Verse 2 explains, *"By this you know the Spirit of God: Every spirit that confesses that Jesus Christ has come in the flesh is of God."* If a doctrine does not acknowledge that Jesus the Messiah has come in the flesh, that constitutes a false doctrine. Verse 3 continues, *"Every spirit that does not confess that Jesus Christ has come in the flesh is not of God. And this is the spirit of the Antichrist, which you have heard was coming, and is now already in the world."*

1. THE ANTICHRIST WILL ORIGINATE IN THE CHURCH

What distinctive marks will characterize the spirit of antichrist, which will accompany the Antichrist and win people to his side? One answer is found in 1 John 2:19:

They [antichrists] went out from us, but they were not of us; for if they had been of us, they would have continued with us; but they

THE SPIRIT OF ANTICHRIST CAN

OPERATE ONLY WHERE CHRIST

HAS BEEN PROCLAIMED.

went out that they might be made manifest, that none of them were of us.

This passage indicates that a distinctive mark of the spirit of antichrist is that it originates with the backslidden people of God. It cannot originate in paganism—which worships idols and false gods—because opposing God necessitates knowing about Him, and pagan religions are by definition ignorant of God.

The spirit of antichrist can operate only where Christ has been proclaimed. This spirit is Satan's last hope, his final attempt to foil God's purposes.

2. THE ANTICHRIST DENIES THE MESSIAH

The second indicator of the spirit of antichrist appears in 1 John 2:22: *"Who is a liar but he who denies that Jesus is the Christ [Messiah]?"* The spirit of antichrist, while aware of Jesus's coming, denies His claim to be Messiah. The above verse also includes the third indicator: *"He is antichrist who denies the Father and the Son."* The spirit of antichrist rejects the biblically revealed persons of the Godhead: Father and Son.

3. THE ANTICHRIST LEADS PEOPLE TO APOSTASY

Paul gave further insights about the Antichrist and the end of this age in 2 Thessalonians 2:1–4:

Now, brethren, concerning the coming of our Lord Jesus Christ and our gathering together to Him, we ask you, not to be soon shaken in mind or troubled, either by spirit or by word or by letter, as if from us, as though the day of Christ had come. Let no one deceive you by any means; for that Day will not come unless the falling away comes first, and the man of sin is revealed, the son of perdition, who opposes and exalts himself above all that is called God or that is worshipped, so that he sits as God in the temple of God, showing himself that he is God.

In Paul's day, people were already talking about the day of the Lord, so heed the Scriptures and do not believe people who tell you that the day of the Lord has come. The day of the Lord will not arrive, Paul said, until *"the falling away,"* or the apostasy. This means a deliberate rejection of revealed truth. Clearly, this apostasy must occur where truth has already been revealed: in the church.

I believe the apostasy has already begun. The church seems to have started backsliding from the basic truths of the Christian faith affirmed by the Apostles' Creed: that Jesus is the Son of God, that He was conceived of a virgin, that He led a sinless life, that He died an atoning death, that He was buried and raised again from the dead three days later, and that He will come again in power and glory to judge the living and the dead alike.

Throughout the centuries, the church has affirmed these central tenets. But in the past few decades, leaders in the professing church have publicly reneged on these truths. For example, I have the impression that many pastors, priests, and other church leaders do not believe that Jesus was physically resurrected from the dead. Even churches that do not publicly deny canonized truth may have leaders who harbor secret skepticism amounting to apostasy.

Other churches and religions take an increasingly relativistic approach, advocating a universal religion that incorporates components of every religion. Some people favor combining the three monotheistic religions—Christianity, Islam, and Judaism. This would be convenient, except for the fact that Jesus said, *"I am the way, the truth, and the life. No one comes to the Father except through Me"* (John 14:6). This claim—that Jesus is the exclusive way to salvation—offends many people today.

THE ROLE OF DECEPTION

To win worshippers to himself, Satan uses deception. Deception is something to which all are susceptible; no one should assume he or she is immune to it. As we have seen, those who withstand deception—and the sufferings inflicted by Satan—will receive eternal life. Adverse pressures will tempt us to stray from the faith, *"But he who endures to the end shall be saved"* (Matthew 24:13).

In a sense, the devil proves useful for God's purposes: God will use the devil's persecution of Christians to weed out uncommitted individuals so that the truly committed will stand. As Christ's bride, the church must be glorious, holy, spotless, and without blemish. Tremendous opposition will test and purify the church to prepare her for her wedding day, for union with her Bridegroom.

THE ROLE OF PRIDE

Satan also employs pride to win people's worship. Specifically, the movement known as humanism plays an instrumental role in cultivating confidence in human ability and talent. The motto of humanism is, "Man is the measure of all things." Denying an omnipotent deity, this movement deifies man and makes him the ultimate creature with unlimited capacity for knowledge.

Humanism rides the tide of the New Age movement, which denies all absolutes and embraces all philosophies and systems of thought under an umbrella of relativism. This movement rejects the cornerstone on which the Bible—and all truth—is built: *"In the beginning God created the heavens and the earth"* (Genesis 1:1). God was the beginning, not man; He is the measure of all things, not man.

One final point about Satan's deception stems from Revelation 16:13: *"I saw three unclean spirits like frogs coming out of the mouth of the dragon, out of the mouth of the beast, and out of the mouth of the false prophet."* Here we find a satanic trinity that opposes the Holy Trinity: the dragon (versus God the Father), the beast (versus Jesus Christ the Son), and the false prophet (versus the Holy Spirit).

As the ape of God, Satan can never create anything; he is utterly incapable of producing anything original. He can, however, corrupt and distort God's creation, hence his own counterfeit trinity of dragon,

As Christ's bride, the church must be glorious, holy, spotless, and without blemish. Tremendous opposition will test and purify the church to prepare her for her wedding day, for union with her Bridegroom.

beast, and false prophet. This unholy trinity corrupts God's church to make a counterfeit version: the false church, or the harlot.

OUR ULTIMATE GOAL

Our ultimate goal is Christ's righteousness, which He alone imparts through the Holy Spirit. As Proverbs 4:18 teaches, *"But the path of the just [*"righteous"* NIV] is like the shining sun, that shines ever brighter unto the perfect day."*

If we are walking the pathway of the righteous, the light should grow brighter every day as we grow closer to God. If the light by which I live today is no brighter than it was yesterday, I am in danger of backsliding, of relying on self-made methods and rules instead of God's righteousness. This type of backsliding promotes self-righteousness, which must be avoided if we want to prevent spiritual blindness and subsequent deception.

DEFEATING SATAN'S DECEPTIVE SCHEMES

You must make an honest self-evaluation to gauge the degree to which you are susceptible to deception, for only then can you arm yourself against Satan's tactics. These characteristics are not exhaustive, but are rather the most prominent features of people who are most likely to be deceived.

CHARACTERISTICS OF CANDIDATES

1. RELIANCE ON SUBJECTIVE IMPRESSIONS

Subjective impressions—formed from emotions, intuition, and senses—generate conclusions that are often ill-founded and incorrect. Subjective evaluations are highly suspect, skewed by our sinful nature and biased minds.

Someone might say, "When so-and-so prophesied for me, I felt so good. His message must have been from God." This type of evaluation is dangerous because it stems solely from sentiment. Many tests are more important than how you feel about something.

2. COMPLETE TRUST OF HUMAN LEADERS

Some people place complete trust in human leaders, whether they are pastors, priests, prophets, or spiritual mentors. No human leader is infallible. Believing everything anyone says without checking it against Scripture or testing it in other ways is dangerous.

3. ACCEPTANCE OF SUPERNATURAL SIGNS AS A GUARANTEE OF TRUTH

Jesus Himself said that false prophets will arise and perform great signs and wonders—the key word is *false*. The mere fact that a sign is supernatural does not suffice as a guarantee of its authenticity.

False prophets exist, and Satan is capable of supernatural signs and wonders, too. As we have discussed, anyone who accepts these things blindly and assumes they come from God is sure to succumb to deception.

4. UNWILLINGNESS TO FACE SUFFERING OR PERSECUTION

The Bible warns us that as believers, we must expect to face persecution and suffering for our faith. Peter wrote, *"Since Christ suffered for us in the flesh, arm yourselves also with the same mind, for he who has suffered in the flesh has ceased from sin, that he no longer should live the rest of his time in the flesh for the lusts of men, but for the will of God"* (1 Peter 4:1–2).

Second Timothy 3:12 likewise tells us, *"All who desire to live godly in Christ Jesus will suffer persecution."* Suffering is a reality of the Christian life. God uses it to shape us. Anyone who expects or promises only good things is a false prophet or a misled individual.

5. IGNORANCE OF SCRIPTURE

Some people in remote, unreached countries do not have a Bible; they have only a word—perhaps the teachings of missionaries or a spoken explanation of the gospel. God will be merciful to them. But for those of us who have Bibles at our ready disposal, neglecting to study them sets us up for deception. By arming ourselves with the truth as expressed in God's Word, we can avoid much deception. But if we remain ignorant about His truths and teachings, we deserve to be deceived.

A SERIES OF SAFEGUARDS

Now that you have a better understanding of what makes people susceptible to deception, you will be more equipped to recognize false-hoods and resist deception. To foil the schemes of Satan, practice the following four safeguards when you are tempted by pride, when you encounter signs and wonders, or when your awe of God wanes.

These safeguards, paired with a close, personal relationship with Christ, will guard you from deception and enable you to maintain your membership in the true church.

1. HUMILITY

The first safeguard may be found in 1 Peter 5:5–6: *"'God resists the proud, but gives grace to the humble.' Therefore humble yourselves under the mighty hand of God, that He may exalt you in due time."* Humility consists in exalting God and putting others first rather than seeking to exalt ourselves. This quality is essential if we expect to come into the presence of God.

HUMILITY CONSISTS IN
EXALTING GOD AND PUTTING
OTHERS FIRST RATHER THAN
SEEKING TO EXALT OURSELVES.
THIS QUALITY IS ESSENTIAL IF
WE EXPECT TO COME INTO THE
PRESENCE OF GOD.

The Bible never says that God will make us humble; it is our responsibility. People can preach to us and pray for us, but the ultimate decision to practice humility must be our own. Psalm 25:8–9 provides encouragement: *"Good and upright is the* Lord; *therefore He teaches sinners in the way. The humble He guides in justice, and the humble He teaches His way."* It is thanks to His grace that the Lord teaches sinners at all. God does not enroll students based on intellectual qualifications, but on character. Many people may attend Bible school or seminary, but they cannot register for classes in God's school unless they humble themselves.

2. A LOVE OF THE TRUTH

The second safeguard stems from a warning in 2 Thessalonians 2:9: *"The coming of the lawless one* [the Antichrist] *is according to the working of Satan, with all power, signs, and lying wonders."*

Never underestimate Satan's ability to produce power, signs, and wonders. Many charismatics attribute anything supernatural to God, which is why I have identified the charismatic movement as a likely place for the Antichrist to emerge.

How can we protect ourselves from being deceived by Satan's supernatural signs and wonders? We must receive a love of the truth. In 2 Thessalonians 2:10, we see that *"unrighteous deception"* will ensnare *"those who perish, because they did not receive the love of the truth, that they might be saved."* God offers us a love of the truth, and we must accept it to be saved. Cultivating a love of the truth entails more than reading your Bible daily, going to church, and hearing sermons. It means having a passionate commitment to the truth of God.

To those who reject a love of the truth, 2 Thessalonians 2:11–12 says, *"For this reason God will send them strong delusion, that they should believe the lie, that they all may be condemned who did not believe the truth but had pleasure in unrighteousness."*

When God sends delusion, it deludes without fail. Should He delude someone, there are two possible ways to pray: first, that God will work through the delusion to accomplish His purposes; second, that God will protect us from succumbing to the delusion ourselves.

3. THE FEAR OF THE LORD

The fear of the Lord is crucial in the Christian life. Fear of God, or "fear of the Lord," to the Christian, is a feeling of reverence, awe, and respect of God. The unbeliever has every reason to be panic-stricken in his fear of God because he stands condemned before Him. Psalm 34:11–14 reads,

> *Come, you children, listen to me; I will teach you the fear of the LORD. Who is the man who desires life, and loves many days, that he may see good? Keep your tongue from evil, and your lips from speaking deceit. Depart from evil and do good; seek peace and pursue it.*

Additional Scriptures about the fear of the Lord include Psalm 19:9—"*The fear of the LORD is clean, enduring forever*"—and Job 28:28— "*Behold, the fear of the Lord, that is wisdom, and to depart from evil is understanding.*"

The requirements of the fear of the Lord are not intellectual, but moral. Clever fools abound; we must depart from evil and instead do what is right. Proverbs 8:13 teaches, "*The fear of the LORD is to hate evil; pride and arrogance and the evil way and the perverse mouth I hate.*" The fear of the Lord requires a hatred of evil; you must despise pride and arrogance. In this way, you will not leave the door open for spiritual blindness and deception.

When we value the fear of the Lord, we guard against pride, ingratitude, and taking God for granted.

THE REQUIREMENTS OF THE
FEAR OF THE LORD ARE NOT
INTELLECTUAL, BUT MORAL.
CLEVER FOOLS ABOUND; WE
MUST DEPART FROM EVIL AND
INSTEAD DO WHAT IS RIGHT.

4. A SURRENDER TO THE CENTRALITY OF THE CROSS

In 1 Corinthians 2:1–3, Paul wrote,

I, brethren, when I came to you, did not come with excellence of speech or of wisdom declaring to you the testimony of God. For I determined not to know anything among you except Jesus Christ and Him crucified. I was with you in weakness, in fear, and in much trembling.

In Paul's day, oratory prowess was the utmost achievement; unskilled public speakers were derided and despised. To show that he relied only on Christ and His atoning work on the cross, Paul highlighted his own inability and weakness.

As he emphasized in 2 Corinthians 12:9, God's strength is made perfect in man's weakness. God must bring us to the place where our strength fails so that we learn to rely on the strength He provides. Otherwise, we again will lean on our own perceived sufficiency and may fall into the snares of self-righteousness.

My own ministry testifies to this truth: to use me in any significant way, God had to bring me to the point of incapability, where I acknowledged my dependence upon His strength, perfected in my weakness. When I prepared to preach, I would pray to God, "I know I do not have the ability. I am totally dependent upon You. If You do not anoint me, if You do not inspire me, if You do not strengthen me, I cannot do it."

If we practice the safeguards we have discussed, it will make us less susceptible to deception. In the next chapter, we will continue with some suggestions of ways to keep ourselves from being deceived.

16

CULTIVATING A LIFE IN CHRIST

It goes without saying that a personal relationship with Christ is necessary if we are to thwart the schemes of the devil.

First and foremost, we must cultivate a love of the truth, for in doing so we love God and seek His Word, which is truth.

In 2 Thessalonians 2:9–10, we learn that loving the truth will protect us from the Antichrist:

The coming of the lawless one is according to the working of Satan, with all power, signs, and lying wonders, and with all unrighteous deception among those who perish, because they did not receive the love of the truth, that they might be saved.

If we reject the love of the truth, we are bound to perish. The word *"love"* in this case means more than just tolerating the truth or allowing someone to present the truth to us. It means seeking the truth, finding it for ourselves.

We must take time to read our Bibles and to bask in the presence of the Lord. Time spent in His presence equips us to recognize the truth and to reject everything else.

GIVE GOD YOUR TIME

Spending time in fellowship with other Christians is important, but more important still is spending time alone with God. Many people devote a negligible amount of time to God. They should repent and change their ways.

My wife Ruth and I regularly took one day each week—we chose Wednesday—to wait on God. We had no preconceived notions of what would happen; we had neither agenda nor prayer list. Sometimes we would begin by reading the Bible; other times we would not. But by the end of the day, we always asked, "How did we ever get here?" God always surprised us with where we were and what we were doing at the end of the day.

At one point, Ruth and I took a six-month sabbatical from November to April. We went to Hawaii, deeming it an appropriate place to be renewed and refreshed. We had just finished a certain phase of our life and ministry, having passed the reins of Derek Prince Ministries to David Selby, his competent staff, and the board of directors. Waiving all responsibilities except prayer, we headed to Hawaii with the purpose of seeking God's direction and trusting Him to prepare and equip us for the next phase. We made no commitments; I did no preaching.

What we anticipated as a relaxing time turned into one of the most difficult and trying periods I have ever endured. My health declined significantly; I spent two and a half weeks in a hospital with a heart condition that was, until recently, incurable. Had it escaped diagnosis, I might have died in Hawaii. I thank God for providing doctors, nurses, and medical treatment, as well as people to support and pray for us.

During this time, God provided a clear sense of the direction our ministry was to take: from then on, we were first and foremost to engage in intercession, prayer, worship, and waiting on God. This final instruction—waiting on God—was an appropriate lesson learned by doing just that. Had we set aside only four or five months for our sabbatical, we might not have received an answer. For five and a half months, God was silent about the answer. He taught us many things, but it was not until the last two weeks that He revealed the answer to what we were seeking to know.

God's other lessons to us during the sabbatical dealt with time as well. God wants our time, and if we refuse to devote time to Him, I do not think we should expect to hear from Him. God wants not just any time, but open-ended time. Instead of saying, "Lord, we will give You the next half-hour or the next half-day," we should say, "Lord, we will give You time until we hear from You, no matter how long it takes."

Many people are impatient to hear from God. You might ask, "Why did you have to wait five and a half months to hear from God?" First, God is sovereign: He does what He wants, when He wants, the way He wants. He does not require our permission or sanction. He answers in His timing. Second, God revealed to us many personal, internal barriers we needed to dismantle before He could speak and show us His way. He took five and a half months to deal with those barriers, leading us through a process of confession, repentance, and self-humbling. Self-humbling is often crucial; it is an action rather than a feeling.

Someone once said, "Humility is not something you are; humility is something you do." Rather than trying to feel humble, we must practice humility by putting others first and thinking of our needs as less important. The results will follow.

BE HUMBLE

I have already emphasized the importance of humility, which comes when we remove the barrier of pride—a barrier that can inhibit communication with God. One way to humble ourselves before God is by confessing our sins.

1. CONFESS TO GOD

In 1 John 1:9, we read, *"If we confess our sins, He is faithful and just to forgive us our sins and to cleanse us from all unrighteousness."* God does not want to hold your sins against you, which is why He provided a way for you to receive complete cleansing and forgiveness.

There is one condition, however: we must confess our sins. If we do not confess them, they still count against us. Our sole escape is through confession, acknowledging the ways we have wronged God.

I want to discourage you, however, from launching a process of painstaking self-examination, for the more you examine yourself, the less you will like yourself. God has provided an examiner: the Holy Spirit. Jesus said that when the Holy Spirit comes, He will convict us of sin, of righteousness, and of judgment. As John wrote in 1 John 5:17, *"All unrighteousness is sin."* Anything that is not righteousness is, by default, sinful. The distinction is black and white, with no gray area; the Holy Spirit convicts us of anything that is not righteousness. The Holy Spirit does not, however, cause us to feel guilty; only Satan instills guilt and makes us doubt whether we have done enough to compensate for our sin.

2. CONFESS TO OTHERS

The second key to humility is found in James 5:16: *"Confess your trespasses to one another, and pray for one another, that you may be healed."*

HUMILITY COMES WHEN WE
REMOVE THE BARRIER OF
PRIDE—A BARRIER THAT CAN
INHIBIT COMMUNICATION
WITH GOD.

In the Christian life, unconfessed sins pile up and prevent us from receiving healing. We can humble ourselves by confessing our sins to God, and sometimes more so by confessing them to other people. This self-humbling is healthy and is based on scriptural instruction. My wife Ruth and I confessed many things to one another; I believe neither one of us withheld any known sin from the other.

Some years ago I was counseling a man who was unreasonably angry with his wife and children. He was a Christian who earnestly desired to serve and obey the Lord. I recommended that every time he lost his temper, he confess that specific sin to them; the more he did that, the less likely he would be to lose his temper again. I believe many marriages would benefit from the shared confession of sins between husband and wife. Acknowledging wrongdoing and apologizing for it humbles the wrongdoer and heals the heart of the victim.

3. SUBMIT TO GOD'S DEALINGS

A third way to humble ourselves is to submit to God's dealings. In Deuteronomy 32:3–4, Moses proclaimed, *"Ascribe greatness to our God. He is the Rock, His work is perfect; for all His ways are justice, a God of truth and without injustice; righteous and upright is He."* God is just; it is impossible for Him to be either unjust or unfair. Let us not deceive ourselves by thinking that He owes us something. God makes no mistakes, and we cannot call Him unfair just because He fails to fulfill our hopes and desires.

We will all experience "unfair" situations in life. We may lack sufficient financial resources; our friends may betray us. How are we to respond? In 1 Peter 5:6, we are told, *"Humble yourselves under the mighty hand of God, that He may exalt you in due time."* Instead of presuming to know what is best for us and growing bitter when something else happens, we must humble ourselves.

We must pray to God, "Father, I do not understand what is happening, but I know You are perfectly just. You never make mistakes. What

GOD MAKES NO MISTAKES,

AND WE CANNOT CALL HIM

UNFAIR JUST BECAUSE

HE FAILS TO FULFILL OUR

HOPES AND DESIRES.

You do is right, and I submit to Your dealings. Teach me what I do not know, and help me to understand Your ways."

When God brought Israel out of Egypt, He allowed them to pass through great trials designed to humble them. In Deuteronomy 8:2–3, Moses said,

> You shall remember that the LORD your God led you all the way these forty years in the wilderness, to humble you and test you, to know what was in your heart, whether you would keep His commandments or not. So He humbled you, allowed you to hunger, and fed you with manna which you did not know nor did your fathers know.

God allowed the Israelites to them pass through times of apparent need and insufficiency, when their carnal desires were not satisfied. His purpose was to humble them, but the process was prolonged—instead of humbling themselves, one generation perished in the wilderness because they complained, muttered, rebelled, and ultimately blamed God.

When we encounter a difficult time, we must not mutter or whine; nor should we accuse God of unfairness, or we will miss His purpose. If we humble ourselves, God's purposes will be fulfilled.

When my first wife, Lydia, and I had to emigrate from Israel to Britain, we were homeless; our eight girls were divided among different homes, and we were miserable. God spoke, though, and said, "Humble yourselves under the mighty hand of God." It took some time to follow this order, but the result was beneficial. When things go wrong and our wishes are not fulfilled, we should humble ourselves. We must acknowledge God's fairness and ask Him to show us the way of obedience.

Job 7:17–18 is an amazing passage of Scripture addressed to the Lord: "*What is man, that You should exalt him, that You should set Your heart on him, that You should visit him every morning, and test him every moment?*" We undergo continual testing to determine whether we are faithful and obedient or rebellious and disobedient. God tests us every moment and visits us every morning; we must remain open to His guidance.

FOUR NECESSARY CHANGES

These words from Isaiah 40:3–5 about preparing the way for Jesus—which John the Baptist quoted from in John 1:23—prove an appropriate closing to this topic:

> *The voice of one crying in the wilderness: "Prepare the way of the LORD; make straight in the desert a highway for our God. Every valley shall be exalted and every mountain and hill brought low; the crooked places shall be made straight and the rough places smooth; the glory of the LORD shall be revealed, and all flesh shall see it together; for the mouth of the LORD has spoken."*

Just as John the Baptist quoted from these words as he prepared people for Jesus's first coming, I believe God speaks these words to us to prepare us for Jesus's return. This passage ends with the promise that the glory of the Lord will be revealed, and all flesh will see it. How do we prepare the way of the Lord? We must remove the barriers that we erect to resist God's purpose and plans.

Four changes must occur, illustrated by the landscape imagery: (1) Every valley shall be exalted; (2) every mountain and hill shall be brought down; (3) the crooked places shall be made straight; (4) the rough places shall be made smooth. What is low must be raised up; what is high must be reduced. Our hype and exaggeration, our self-aggrandizement and boasting, must cease; we must practice humility. Self-exaltation and self-promotion will hardly hasten God's arrival. He will reward virtues that contemporary society seems to despise: modesty, chastity, self-effacement, servitude.

Any crookedness in our lives must be straightened; rough places must be smoothed. Our egoism, our tendency to react resentfully when things run against what we prefer, our argumentativeness—these should be ironed out.

PREPARING TO BE USEFUL TO GOD

As we undergo trials—personally as individuals, collectively as a church—God prepares us to receive the revelation of His glory, which will occur because His Word says so, and He is faithful to fulfill His Word. His glory will be revealed only through those who have met His conditions—conditions established in the Scripture passage above.

I believe God is working to bring about the fulfillment of this Scripture. More specifically, He is working to bring it about in the church of this nation. We must choose to be either channels for His glory or mountains that withstand it. A time of testing is upon us; in fact, it has started in the lives of many whom God has tested with trials and tribulations.

God never uses anything or anyone without initial testing, so if we want to be of use in His kingdom, we must expect to undergo and pass a test. Let us resolve to persevere through tests, keeping in mind the blessings that will follow if we make the grade. We should not lose determination or drop out, but should rather expect tests and rely on God's grace to pass them.

LIVING IN THE
PRESENT EVIL AGE

In the last two chapters, we learned how to avoid being susceptible to deception by practicing a series of safeguards against Satan's schemes and preparing ourselves to be used by God in the times in which we live. The ultimate protection from deception will occur when Jesus returns again, His kingdom reigns over all the earth, and Satan is cast out forever.

As we will learn, the Bible describes the period of human history that leads up to this time as *"this present evil age"* (Galatians 1:4). This is the age in which we are currently living. In our final chapters, we will learn more about the nature of the present age, how it will culminate with Christ's return, and how to remain faithful to God until the dawn of this day.

ARE WE DIFFERENT?

Until the end of this age arrives, we are to await Christ's coming and to resist deception. How many of us are truly prepared for the end? I fear that a great number of people in America who claim to be born-again Christians are making a regrettably poor impression. When John the Baptist introduced Jesus and the gospel, he said, *"Even now the ax is laid to the root of the trees"* (Matthew 3:10; Luke 3:9).

When God deals with a situation, He does not bother with the branches or the trunk. No, He goes straight for the root. When you deal with the root, you no longer have problems with the tree that grows from it.

Someone gave me a secular publication produced by a reputable marketing research firm. The publication had no spiritual overtones or religious themes; its sole concerns were dollars and cents. The research this publication dealt with was none other than "How to Market to Born-Again Christians." It addressed questions such as these: "What must one say and do to market to Christians? How can you persuade them to make purchases? After all, so-called born-again Christians compose a significant sector of the buying market."

As I read this survey, which spanned about four pages, I could tell that the analyst had spent significant time in close quarters with born-again Christians. He knew exactly what he was talking about.

The ultimate message of the survey is that there is no significant difference between born-again Christian consumers and others who are not in this category. Distinctions were negligible, according to the research, conclusions, and counsel of this highly qualified, secular observer.

WHEN GOD DEALS WITH A
SITUATION, HE GOES STRAIGHT
FOR THE ROOT. WHEN YOU
DEAL WITH THE ROOT, YOU NO
LONGER HAVE PROBLEMS WITH
THE TREE THAT GROWS FROM IT.

A DISTURBING CONCLUSION

This reality should be disturbing to us. As Christians, we are to be in the world, but not of the world. (See John 17:14–16.) Should not our passions, practices, and purpose mark us as radically different from people who do not profess our faith, people who love the world and think that nothing exists beyond it?

A simple illustration provides a pithy parallel to our situation: a ship in the sea is all right; the sea in a ship is all wrong. In the same way, the church in the world is all right; the world in the church is all wrong. If there is too much of the sea in a ship, it will sink. I believe the ship of today's church is so near sinking that every individual who becomes a believer and accepts Christianity is set to bailing water with everyone else to keep the church afloat.

Many of us come to church with needs. If we focus merely on our needs, we will never come to the end of them; rather, we will live with them forever. Something must release us from a myopic focus on our own needs, drawing us beyond the realm of "I need, I want, help me, pray for me, bless me." As long as we dwell on such things, we remain enslaved by them. We need to press past a self-centered focus to acquire the wisdom of God.

The ultimate purpose of everything is not related to us; it is related to God, who is both beginning and end. The world may not recognize this truth, but we, as Christians, do, and should reflect the centrality of God in the way we live.

I believe the church needs a total revolution. God remembers the faithfulness of the ancestors of the American people. I think this generation has spent just about all of its spiritual inheritance, and it is time for God to receive a return on His investment.

THIS WORLD IS ENDING

Let us look once more at a passage in the book of Galatians, where Paul wrote,

THE ULTIMATE PURPOSE OF

EVERYTHING IS NOT RELATED TO

US; IT IS RELATED TO GOD, WHO

IS BOTH BEGINNING AND END.

Grace to you and peace from God the Father and our Lord Jesus Christ, who gave Himself for our sins, that He might deliver us from this present evil age, according to the will of our God and Father.
(Galatians 1:3–4)

Do we understand why it is imperative for us to be delivered from this present evil age? Our deliverance is already taking place, but we must make our calling sure. (See 2 Peter 1:10.) We do not belong to this age; we belong to the next age. Let us consider the solemn truths written in Hebrews 6:4–6:

For it is impossible for those who were once enlightened, and have tasted the heavenly gift, and have become partakers of the Holy Spirit, and have tasted the good word of God and the powers of the age to come, if they fall away, to renew them again to repentance, since they crucify again for themselves the Son of God, and put Him to an open shame.

This passage raises many theological issues, but I personally believe what it says. It is possible to come to a point where one has forfeited any further hope in Christ. I think this applies not only to backsliders, but also to people who turn and actually deny Jesus Christ, even after having known Him, and treat Him irreverently.

This passage speaks of people who have had several experiences. They have been enlightened. The Holy Spirit has shown them the truth. They have tasted the heavenly gift (which is the gift of eternal life in Jesus Christ). They have become partakers of the Holy Spirit. Through faith in Jesus they have received the Holy Spirit. They have tasted the Word of God and have known its truth, reality, and power to nourish and sustain.

The passage then mentions *"the powers of the age to come."* When we are baptized in the Holy Spirit, we begin to taste a small part of what will be normal in the next age. What we call supernatural in this age will be natural in the next age. God gives us a foretaste so that we have an idea of what it will be like.

The dividing line between the true church and the false church at the end of this age will not be determined by whether we speak in tongues. Rather, it will be a matter of faithfulness to the Bridegroom. Have we been faithful or unfaithful? As was discussed in earlier chapters, we will either be the bride—a member of the true church—or the harlot—a member of the false church. No alternatives exist.

AVOIDING CONFORMITY TO THE WORLD

The Bible teaches clearly that we must not conform to the present age. In Romans 12:2, Paul wrote, *"Do not be conformed to this world, but be transformed by the renewing of your mind, that you may prove what is that good and acceptable and perfect will of God."*

As long as we think the same way this age thinks, we cannot discern the will of God for our lives. Countless Christians are stumbling around, wondering what God has in store for them. They fail to find it because they think the way the world thinks. They share the world's values, motives, priorities, and standards. God does not reveal His will to such minds.

1. SELF-CENTEREDNESS

The natural mind is self-centered. It always asks, "What will I get out of this? What will this do for me? What will people say about me?" The renewed mind, on the other hand, is God-centered. It always asks, "Will this please God? Will this glorify Him? Will this expand the kingdom of God?"

As long as we remain self-centered, we are prisoners of ourselves. Adopting a God-centered mind liberates us from slavery to selfishness and allows us to seek the glory of His kingdom.

I have counseled many people who required frequent deliverance. Do you know what I discovered? People who have numerous and persistent problems with demons are typically self-centered. They will spout off their problems without realizing that, by doing so, they are constructing the bars of their own cages. Their primary problem is self-centeredness.

This issue has also caused the breakup of many marriages between so-called Christians. When two spouses are self-centered, their marriage cannot stand, for both ask, "What will I get out of this? What will my spouse do for me?" By asking these questions, they fail to meet the conditions for a successful Christian marriage. Christian marriages begin with a life laid down for one's mate. This self-sacrifice must be mutual. Many marriages of Christians—even of Christian pastors—are breaking down because of the presence of the world within the church.

2. WORRIES

In the parable of the sower in the book of Matthew, we read, *"He who received seed among the thorns is he who hears the word, and the cares of this world and the deceitfulness of riches choke the word, and he becomes unfruitful"* (Matthew 13:22). We learn here that one characteristic of this age is that it impresses cares and worries on us.

These worries, while sometimes trifling, are nonetheless significant because they can keep us from being ready to meet the Lord. In Luke 21:34, Jesus said, *"But take heed to yourselves, lest your hearts be weighed down with carousing, drunkenness, and cares of this life."* Such cares command our attention and distract our focus, preventing us from being prepared for the next age.

3. PETTY, FRIVOLOUS RULES

In my experience with the Pentecostal tradition, I became intimately familiar with its set of rules: clothing you must not wear, places you must not go. Many people who observe these rules still react to situations as the world does. While they have changed a few minor external details, such as fashion and pastimes, their thinking has not changed in the slightest.

When God changes someone, He does not start with the exterior, giving commands to remove makeup or to wear long dresses. Instead, He starts with the interior, changing the way people think. Once He changes our thinking, He does not have to worry about our conduct; it will align naturally with our thinking.

4. LOVE OF THE WORLD

A final problem in our dealing with the present age is discussed in 2 Timothy. Paul instructed Timothy, *"Be diligent to come to me quickly; for Demas has forsaken me, having loved this present world, and has departed for Thessalonica"* (2 Timothy 4:9–10).

What was Demas's problem? He loved the present age. From two additional epistles, we know that Demas had been a trusted coworker of the apostle Paul and had been with him through many situations. Paul was clearly unaware of this character flaw, so he must have been quite shocked to learn of Demas's love for this world.

Demas probably had a long list of reasons to break company with Paul: Paul was getting old and growing feeble; he was in jail; the days when he had stirred entire cities with his sermons had passed. One of his closest associates, Trophimus, was ailing, and Paul had left him behind in Miletus, unable to even pray him back to health. By worldly standards, Paul was a failure. Demas measured according to the world's standards, concluding, "This is a sinking ship; I had better get off while I can."

I would not suppose that, having parted company with Paul, Demas entered a life of sin. He was not pursuing prostitutes or frequenting bars. He just wanted a more secure and reasonable kind of life. His mistake was not one we typically preach against. Had he been an abject sinner, Paul would not have kept him as a fellow worker. Demas's one fatal flaw was his love for the present age, but this had been latent for years.

Could it be that we harbor the same love, that we have the same flaw? It is remarkable what people can get by with in the world today, but what the world accepts, God rejects. There will come a time in every life when everyone will be tested, and they will pass, assuming they do not have this fatal weakness of a love for the present age.

We must not condemn Demas unless we are absolutely sure that we would not have done the same thing he did. Suppose we had been with Paul. He is in prison; he is manacled; it is getting cold and wintry... would we have deserted him, too? I believe that if we do not practice laying down our lives daily, we will not lay them down when the big moment arrives. Those who lead self-pleasing, self-centered lives now will not be able to make the right decision when the final moment comes.

18

OVERCOMING THE WORLD

The world does not recognize Jesus or His disciples. As John 1:10 attests, "*He [Jesus] was in the world, and the world was made through Him, and the world did not know Him.*" Why did the world not know Jesus? Because their eyes had been blinded by Satan.

In 1 John 3:1, we read, "*Behold what manner of love the Father has bestowed on us, that we should be called children of God! Therefore the world does not know us, because it did not know Him.*" If the world does not know our elder brother, Jesus, the world does not know the other members of His family.

We should not worry if the world does not know us. It did not know Him, either. In fact, we should worry if the world thinks too well of us. If it does, we may be in danger.

HATED BY THE WORLD

The next statement goes further, saying that the world actually hates Jesus and His followers. In John 15:18–19, Jesus told His disciples,

If the world hates you, you know that it hated Me before it hated you. If you were of the world, the world would love its own. Yet because you are not of the world, but I chose you out of the world, therefore the world hates you.

Notice that in verse 19, the phrase *"the world"* occurs five times. Jesus must have meant what He was saying.

In John 17:14, Jesus prayed for His disciples, saying, *"I have given them Your word; and the world has hated them because they are not of the world, just as I am not of the world."*

Brothers and sisters, we must not worry if the world hates us. Rather, we should take heart, because if the world loved us as its own, we would belong in the wrong company. I do not mean to suggest that we go around looking for persecution. But I do mean that we must be realistic: sooner or later, the world will hate us.

OPPOSITE SPIRITS

The Spirit of God and the world are completely at odds with one another. First Corinthians 2:11 says, *"What man knows the things of a man except the spirit of the man which is in him? Even so no one knows the things of God except the Spirit of God."* The sole source of revelation of the things of God is the Holy Spirit.

Paul continued in verse 12, *"Now we have received, not the spirit of the world, but the Spirit who is from God, that we might know the things that have been freely given to us by God."* It is not the spirit of the world, but rather the Spirit of God, who makes known to us the things of God. The spirit of the world and the Spirit of God are opposites.

In 1 Corinthians 2:13, we read, *"These things we also speak, not in words which man's wisdom teaches but which the Holy Spirit teaches, comparing spiritual things with spiritual."* This verse is significant. No human discipline—such as philosophy, psychology, or psychiatry—acknowledges the reality of the Spirit. But man is spirit, soul, and body. Any attempt to classify man that excludes the reality of the spirit distorts the truth.

When I hear preachers quote famous psychologists, I sometimes fear what they will say. God's Word does not need to be endorsed by psychologists or psychiatrists. It does its own job. God's Word is alive, powerful, and sharper than any two-edged sword. It divides soul from spirit; in fact, it is the only thing that can do so.

Hebrews 4:12 says,

For the word of God is living and powerful, and sharper than any two-edged sword, piercing even to the division of soul and spirit, and of joints and marrow, and is a discerner of the thoughts and intents of the heart.

GOD'S SPIRIT IS GREATER

The good news is that the Spirit of God in believers is greater than the spirit of the world. Hallelujah! First John 4:1–6 says,

Beloved, do not believe every spirit, but test the spirits, whether they are of God; because many false prophets have gone out into the world. By this you know the Spirit of God: Every spirit that confesses that Jesus Christ has come in the flesh is of God, and every spirit that does not confess that Jesus Christ has come in the flesh is not of God. And this is the spirit of the Antichrist, which you have heard was coming, and is now already in the world. You are of God, little children, and have overcome them, because He who is in you is greater than he who is in the world. They are of the world. Therefore they speak as of the world, and the world hears them. We are of God. He who knows God hears us; he who is not of God does not hear us. By this we know the spirit of truth and the spirit of error.

"*He who is in you*" is the Holy Spirit. The spirit in the world is the spirit of Antichrist. You and I can thank God that we are on the winning side! While I do not believe we are going to take over the world, I do believe we will not be defeated by Satan. Worldly people hear the spirit of this world. We must present the truth in the power of the Holy Spirit, but we cannot meet the world on its own terms.

When we stop being impressed by what the world thinks, and when we stop adhering to the world's standards and values, we cease to be slaves to the world. What a liberating experience! Instead of working to please the world, we can live to please God. Now, I do not advise going out of your way to offend people; I believe we should be gracious, tactful, and humble, but we should not bow to the god of this world.

FOCUS ON THE ETERNAL

As we read in 1 Corinthians 2:12–14, the Spirit of God reveals the things of God. But the spirit of the world ridicules the things of God, which are foolishness to anyone who lacks the Spirit. In John 16:13–14, Jesus said that when the Spirit of truth has come, "*He will glorify Me.*" This is a foolproof test of whether the Holy Spirit is at work. Is the movement or method under consideration glorifying to Jesus? If not, we can be sure that it is not of the Spirit of God.

The spirit of the world focuses on man, preparing the world for the Antichrist. The philosophy of humanism fuels this focus on man; it holds that man is the measure of all things, and that nothing higher than man exists, making man equal to a god.

WHEN WE STOP BEING IMPRESSED
BY WHAT THE WORLD THINKS,
AND WHEN WE STOP ADHERING
TO THE WORLD'S STANDARDS
AND VALUES, WE CEASE TO BE
SLAVES TO THE WORLD.

Hebrews 9:14 says, *"Christ…through the eternal Spirit offered Himself without spot to God."* The Holy Spirit is the *"eternal Spirit"*; the Greek word for this term means spirit of all the ages, a spirit that is not limited or bounded by time.

Second Timothy 1:7 says, *"God has not given us a spirit of fear, but of power and of love and of a sound mind."* The *"power"* this passage refers to is not political, physical, or military; rather, it is spiritual power—power over evil. The spirit of this world is the spirit of subjection to evil, but the Spirit of God brings love to overpower evil. The spirit of this world brings strife, disharmony, and hatred. Yet Hebrews 10:29 calls the Holy Spirit the *"Spirit of grace."*

The only way that grace enters our lives is through God's Holy Spirit. The spirit of this world is the opposite of grace; it is the spirit of fleshly effort, the spirit of people who struggle, practice self-reliance, and believe they can pull themselves up by their own bootstraps.

To summarize, the spirit of this world, the *"spirit of error"* (1 John 4:6), completely opposes the Spirit of God, the Spirit of truth. The Spirit of God reveals the things of God—truths that are mocked and reviled by the spirit of this world. The spirit of this world focuses on man, but the Spirit of God focuses on Jesus. The Spirit of God convicts of sin, righteousness, and judgment, while the spirit of this world denies the real and lasting significance of these things. One day, we all will give an account to God. Praise Him who makes us righteous.

THE SPIRIT OF THIS WORLD

FOCUSES ON MAN,

BUT THE SPIRIT OF GOD

FOCUSES ON JESUS.

AVOIDING THE
CORRUPTION OF LUST

As we saw earlier, overcoming the world means not being corrupted by the world's lusts. Second Peter 1:3–4 says:

> [God's] *divine power has given to us all things that pertain to life and godliness, through the knowledge of Him who called us by glory and virtue, by which have been given to us exceedingly great and precious promises, that through these you may be partakers of the divine nature, having escaped the corruption that is in the world through lust.*

OUR DIVINE DESTINY

In this passage, we learn that we will not have to ask God for anything; He has given it already. All we must do is discover the promises and claim them, because they are there for the taking. *"Through these [the promises of God's Word] you may be partakers of the divine nature [the nature of God Himself], having escaped the corruption that is in the world through lust."*

Our divine destiny is to become partakers of the nature of God, and to do so more and more. The more of God's Word we take in, the more we acquire the nature of God, thus partaking of His nature. The more we partake of God's nature, the less likely we are to become corrupt, because the divine nature cannot accommodate corruption; they are completely incompatible.

In the New Testament, lust is a word with a specific meaning: perverted, inordinate desires. Man was created with only good desires, but when he turned against his Creator and rebelled, those good desires were perverted. The gratification of these perverse desires leads to corruption.

In 1 John 2:15, we are instructed, *"Do not love the world or the things in the world. If anyone loves the world, the love of the Father is not in him."* We cannot love both the world and the Father. This is an issue of either-or, for love of the world and love of God are mutually exclusive. Verse 16 continues, *"For all that is in the world; the lust of the flesh, the lust of the eyes, and the pride of life; is not of the Father but is of the world."* Again, the love of Father and love of the world are incompatible.

THREE ASPECTS OF LUST

In 1 John 2:17, we read, *"The world is passing away, and the lust of it; but he who does the will of God abides forever."* The world is corrupt through lust, three types of which John delineated in verse 16: the lust of the flesh, the lust of the eyes, and the pride of life.

An analysis of temptation as it is recorded throughout the Bible shows that it takes these three forms—lust of the flesh, lust of the eyes, or the pride of life. Temptation began with Eve, when Satan enticed her to taste the forbidden fruit. Genesis 3:6 says, *"When the woman **saw** that the tree was good for food, that it was **pleasant to the eyes**, and a tree desirable to make one wise, she took of its fruit and ate"* (emphasis added).

The beginning of Eve's problem was her moving out of the realm of faith and into the realm of the senses. Instead of believing what God had said, she went by what she saw. This precipitated her downfall. The only way back is the inverse: renouncing the guidance of fallible senses and believing instead the Word of God.

Eve's temptation corresponds to the lusts specified in 1 John 2:16: *"good for food"* (lust of the flesh), *"pleasant to the eyes"* (lust of the eyes), and *"desirable to make one wise"* (the pride of life; the desire to exalt oneself). If we analyze the nature of this temptation, we will find that it was not a temptation to do evil, per se. The temptation was to be like God.

INDEPENDENCE FROM GOD

The essence of this temptation was the desire for independence from God. As long as we desire in our hearts to be independent of God, we occupy a dangerous position. Nothing in this created universe has any right to be independent of its Creator, God.

Adam and Eve believed they could achieve independence by gaining knowledge. The desire to know was not wrong, in itself, but the desire to know as a means of gaining independence was the root of their problem. I know many Christians who have not dealt with the desire to be independent of God.

The pride of life causes individuals to say, "I can manage my life without God. If I am in a real emergency, I may pray, but in general, I can handle the situation." Some people treat the Holy Spirit like an emergency vehicle or 9-1-1 number. When all else fails, they pray. This is not the way we were designed to live. We were designed to live in an hour-by-hour, moment-by-moment dependence on the Spirit of God.

THE PROCESS OF CORRUPTION

An additional point of interest is that Adam fell through eating, while Jesus overcame by fasting. When we have dealt with our stomachs, we have dealt with the root. Fasting, when rightly practiced, is effective for spiritual growth.

When I was saved, I knew I had to fast; I did so every Wednesday for four and a half years. I do not believe I could have ever become what God intended me to be without learning, early on, the secret of fasting.

We must therefore avoid the corruption of lust that controls the world. When something becomes corrupt, it is impossible to eradicate the corruption, be it fruit, flesh, or anything else. Consider, for example, a Georgia peach. If you put it on a shelf and leave it there for one week, it will begin to wither and turn yellow, losing its pleasant aroma and flavor. Once this happens, you cannot reverse the process or restore the fruit's freshness. You can put the peach in the refrigerator to slow the corruption process, but you still cannot reverse it.

I think some churches act like refrigerators, slowing but not stopping the corruption of the fruit they contain—their congregations. The corruption may not be rapid or glaring, but it is still there. This is true of the world, too; there is nothing to reverse the process of corruption.

God is not going to change the world; He is going to replace the world. This is what He does in our lives. Sin corrupts us, so we must be born again. He gives us a new start. He does not patch up or repair our old, corrupted selves; rather, He makes us new beings with a new, divine origin and an incorruptible life. We must live holy lives in keeping with this life.

WHEN SOMETHING BECOMES
CORRUPT, IT IS IMPOSSIBLE TO
ERADICATE THE CORRUPTION,
BE IT FRUIT, FLESH, OR
ANYTHING ELSE.

AVOID CONTAMINATION BY THE WORLD

Believers must use, but not abuse, the world. There can be a fine line between these two words—use and abuse. In 1 Corinthians 7:31, we read, *"Those who use this world as not misusing it. For the form of this world is passing away."* The *New International Version* says, *"Those who use the things of the world, as if not engrossed in them."* In other words, we must not let the world grab hold of us. We should keep the world at arm's length, interacting with it but never allowing it to master or possess us.

As we proclaim the gospel, we must not be contaminated by the world, which contains vast amounts of pollutants—spiritual contaminants. The book of James exhorts us concerning spiritual purity. The Bible has little to say about religion, but it has a lot to say about salvation. The difference is that religion is what people do for God, while salvation is what God does for people.

When it comes to religion, if more people would read James 1:26–27, our churches might be much different. Verse 26 says, *"If anyone among you thinks he is religious, and does not bridle his tongue but deceives his own heart, this one's religion is useless."* It does not matter whether we call ourselves Baptists, Catholics, or Pentecostals—if we do not control our tongues, our religion is without value. Some people may have never realized this before.

In the next chapter, we move from avoiding the corruption of the world to the amazing influence God's people will have upon the world.

As we proclaim the
gospel, we must not be
contaminated by the
world, which contains vast
amounts of pollutants—
spiritual contaminants.

20

THE LIGHT OF THE WORLD

In Matthew 5:14, Jesus told His disciples, *"You are the light of the world."* As I wrote earlier, I believe that the Holy Spirit working through the church is the sole source of light in this darkened world. Do not confuse education or enlightenment with light, because you can be completely educated and still remain in the dark. I can say this with authority because it once applied to me. I had the best education Britain could offer; I was an academic success, but spiritually, I was completely in the dark.

Another important Scripture passage about the church's influence in the world is Philippians 2:15–16, where Paul wrote about his hope,

that you may become blameless and harmless, children of God with-
out fault in the midst of a crooked and perverse generation, among
whom you shine as lights in the world, holding fast the word of life.

The last phrase—*"holding fast the word of life"*—is crucial. We shine
only insofar as we hold forth the *"word of life."* Whatever calling God
gives to each of us, we must shine in these areas, holding forth the word
of life in some measure. As we proclaim the good news, we shed light in
the world and share hope with a dark and perishing generation.

REPRESENTING JESUS

As believers, we are to be Jesus's representatives in the world. I
heard the testimony of a man who served in the British navy during
World War II. He was an adamant unbeliever who was assigned to a
small naval ship with only a few fellow personnel, one of whom was a
Christian. The unbelieving man disliked the Christian and wanted to
keep a distance between them, but there was no place to escape him
on that small ship. The unbeliever would not read his Bible, but he had
no choice but to "read" the life of the Christian man, with whom daily
interaction and intimacy was inevitable. By his life and character, the
Christian man convinced the unbeliever of God's existence.

Remember: you may be the only Bible someone is ever going to read.
There may be someone at your workplace, someone in your neighbor-
hood, or someone at the grocery store who never opens a Bible but who
looks at your life and can see a reflection of God.

First John 4:17 says, *"As He is, so are we in this world."* The world
does not see Jesus, but the world does see us who believe in Him. They
should see us as being as Jesus is.

Not only are we to model Jesus, but we are also to proclaim the
gospel message to the entire world. In Matthew 24:3, the disciples asked
Jesus, *"What will be the sign of Your coming, and of the end of the age?"*

Remember: you may be the only Bible someone is ever going to read.

Notice that they asked to know *"the sign"*—not signs, plural, but *"the sign,"* singular.

In His response in the verses that follow, Jesus gave them a list of signs—among which were *"famines, pestilences, and earthquakes in various places"* (verse 7)—but He had yet to answer the question. In verse 14, He finally concluded, *"This gospel of the kingdom will be preached in all the world as a witness to all the nations, and then the end will come."* This is a specific answer to a specific question.

What will signify the end of the age? The gospel will be proclaimed in all the world as a witness to all the nations. When this has come to pass, the end will follow. Along with the various signs Jesus promised, the tell-tale sign of the end of the age consists of the gospel's being spread throughout the world.

SPREADING THE GOSPEL MESSAGE

Who is responsible for proclaiming the gospel? We are. We must understand that the destiny of many people hinges on us and on what we do. Their eternal destiny is not in the hand of the military leaders, politicians, or scientists. These people cannot bring the end of the age. We alone, as Christians, are responsible.

Recall that Satan is the god of this age. He does not want the age to end, for when it does, he will cease to be a god. Therefore, Satan does everything in his power to delay or postpone the end of the age. We are responsible for seeing that the age is brought to God's appointed climax. We do not do this by merely sitting in church and singing hymns but by proclaiming the gospel. I do not think the devil really objects to most churches. You might think I am being cynical, but I think Satan sees churches as an effective way of keeping most Christians harmlessly and fruitlessly occupied.

Jesus never said to go and make church members of all nations. Instead, He said to make disciples of all nations. (See Matthew 28:19.)

A major problem in the church today is that our churches are filled with members who are not disciples.

Jesus said to go into all the world, preaching the gospel to every creature, and that signs will follow those who believe. They will lay hands on the sick so that they recover, cast out demons, speak with new tongues, and so forth. (See Mark 16:17–18.) I have heard people say that the signs do not actually follow many believers, and this is why: the signs do not follow because the people do not go where God wants them to go. The signs follow those who go, and they have not been promised to any other group, especially a group of stationary people. As the saying goes, "It is hard to follow a parked car."

I once spent nine consecutive days in Pakistan, a country whose population is mostly Muslim. Christians were a tiny, oppressed, despised minority. However, God supernaturally enabled us to hold public meetings. During those nine days, the local Christians estimated that eighty-five hundred people prayed for salvation. At least one-third of these people were Muslims. We saw the most outstanding specific miracles I have ever witnessed in the course of my ministry. Very rarely have I seen the sense of hearing restored to a deaf person, or a crippled person healed, but in Pakistan, I witnessed both of these miracles.

The most incredible miracle of this experience was probably the healing of a Pakistani woman who was about sixty years old—she had been born blind, and she received perfect sight. We did not even lay hands on her; we merely prayed a collective prayer. It was impossible to lay hands on the throngs of people gathered there.

I tell you about this because I want to show, on the basis of personal experience, that signs do follow those who believe and go. You would be surprised what you could achieve with God if you would move out from where you are to a place where no one else goes. The best place for a miracle is the worst of places, for when there is no other way of obtaining results, God will provide a miracle.

I HAVE HEARD PEOPLE SAY THAT

THE SIGNS DO NOT ACTUALLY

FOLLOW MANY BELIEVERS, AND

THIS IS WHY: THE SIGNS DO NOT

FOLLOW BECAUSE THE PEOPLE

DO NOT GO WHERE GOD WANTS

THEM TO GO.

This is the harvest hour. Jesus said to pray that God would send forth laborers into the harvest. (See Matthew 9:38.) The word in Greek for *"send"* means *"thrust,"* and it is the same word in the New Testament used to talk about driving out demons. People must be "driven out" into the harvest by divine pressure. I pray that some of you will never be content until you are in the harvest. That is a challenge. People miss the call of God because they fail to listen.

SERVING THE WORLD

James 1:27 continues, *"Pure and undefiled religion before God and the Father is this: to visit orphans and widows in their trouble, and to keep oneself unspotted from the world."* This is God's view of religion.

How many "religious" people in the United States are practicing this form of *"pure and undefiled religion"*? Brothers and sisters, there is no shortage of orphans or widows. The Third World countries are filled with them. You can help them through one of many organizations that exist to reach out to them.

James 4:17 says, *"Therefore, to him who knows to do good and does not do it, to him it is sin."* I doubt whether God will charge us primarily with our sins of commission. Instead, it will be our sins of omission that He will admonish the most. We may have to sacrifice some personal convenience and give up some of our time. Every now and then, we have to think of someone other than ourselves. What a revolution!

James 1:27 says, *"Visit orphans and widows in their trouble, and...keep oneself unspotted from the world."* The world is dirty. Every time we come in contact with it, we must cleanse ourselves. We must not let any of the dirty, greasy marks of the world soil our beautiful, white robe of righteousness in Christ. If we happen to get a greasy stain on our robes, there is only one detergent that cleans: the blood of Jesus.

Have you ever tried to imagine what it would be like to be guilty and defiled without knowing where to go or what to do? To carry alone on your conscience the fact that you have done things of which you are ashamed, things you wished had never happened?

It is hard enough for a Christian to bear his conscience—and, after all, we can go straight to Jesus, confess, repent, and receive forgiveness, as if the sinful acts we committed never actually happened. Just imagine the agony of countless people burdened by their consciences but not knowing where to go! This is why we must *"preach the gospel to every creature"* (Mark 16:15).

Yet, again, we must interact with the world using discernment. In James 4:4, we read, *"Adulterers and adulteresses! Do you not know that friendship with the world is enmity with God? Whoever therefore wants to be a friend of the world makes himself an enemy of God."*

We cannot be on friendly terms with the system of this world. We can be friendly with our neighbors and show God's love to them, of course, but we must make sure not to fall in love with the system of the world, for it is wicked. The system of the world is controlled by the Prince of Darkness.

Where do we stand today? If you are willing, tell the Lord, "In the light of what Brother Prince has taught, I realize I have not been delivered from this present evil age, and I haven't had an inner transformation in my thinking, my values, or my motives. God, I want You to change me. Whatever it takes, I want You to change me." God will take you at your word.

OVERCOMING THE WORLD

As believers at odds with the world, we are guaranteed to meet with great difficulty. Jesus told His disciples, *"These things I have spoken to you, that in Me you may have peace. In the world you will have tribulation; but be of good cheer, I have overcome the world"* (John 16:33).

In the world, we will have tribulation. We may as well praise the Lord for it, because there will be no alleviation of tribulations if we do not praise Him. A dangerous kind of teaching is spreading that says if you encounter troubles and pressures, it means you are not living aligned with the will of God. This teaching is not necessarily true. When Paul and Barnabas spoke to a group of new converts in the cities they visited, they said, in effect, "Brethren, we must go through much tribulation to enter the kingdom of God. This is a hard fact of the Christian life." (See Acts 14:21–22.)

The guarantee of tribulation entails a piece of good news: through faith, believers have victory over the world.

> *For whatever is born of God overcomes the world. And this is the victory that has overcome the world; our faith. Who is he who overcomes the world, but he who believes that Jesus is the Son of God?*
> (1 John 5:4–5)

The phrase *"overcome the world"* indicates a conflict with the world. We do not overcome something unless it stands in opposition to us. But we overcome the world by our faith when we exercise it.

21

MAINTAINING FOCUS

I have met many Christians who are easily distracted from focusing supremely on God. There are countless ways in which the devil can divert us from God's purpose for our lives. With whatever method works, Satan gets us out of line with God's purposes. Someone may not be a lost soul, but he or she may have a smaller reward in glory than he or she could have had.

Paul wrote to the church in Philippi about finishing his course, completing the objective to which God called him:

I press on, that I may lay hold of that for which Christ Jesus has also laid hold of me. Brethren, I do not count myself to have appre-hended; but one thing I do, forgetting those things which are behind and reaching forward to those things which are ahead, I press toward the goal for the prize of the upward call of God in Christ Jesus.

(Philippians 3:12–14)

I have done extensive biblical study concerning the requirements for fulfilling our calling in Christ, and I contend that they may be summed up in a single word: single-mindedness. If you become double-minded and allow your thinking to be diverted, you will not fulfill your calling.

THE CROSS: OUR MEANS OF ESCAPE

In the mid-1950s I was serving as the pastor of a small Pentecostal congregation in the center of London. Three times weekly, we held street meetings in the middle of London, at a place called Speakers' Corner, Marble Arch. Preaching on the streets provides excellent train-ing because you cannot rely on your notes or outlines. Extemporizing is essential, as is the ability to deal with hecklers and answer questions quickly.

During this period, I had a vivid dream in which I saw a typical street meeting—a circle of people stood and listened to a man in the center of the group. He was preaching with fervor. But as I looked at the man, I did not like what I saw. He was crooked, with a club foot and a hunched back. I said to myself, *What he is saying is good, but I do not like the way he looks.*

When I woke up, I thought nothing more of the dream until it recurred two weeks later. The repetition made me realize that God was trying to tell me something. I began to pray, describing the scene to the Lord and asking Him to identify the preacher. Who was the man? This question was answered in the same way the prophet Nathan answered David: *"Thou art the man"* (2 Samuel 12:7 KJV).

My old man deserved nothing less than the cross, but Jesus took my place. My old man was crucified in Him.

I realized that God was not criticizing my preaching, but He was looking at me, and He did not approve of what He saw. Meanwhile, I had been saved, baptized in the Holy Spirit, and could speak in tongues.

I began to think seriously about this dream. It was about Easter time, so the image of the three crosses on the hill of Golgotha was vivid in my mind. The middle cross was taller than the other two. As I turned this image over in my mind, the Holy Spirit seemed to talk to me, saying, "About that middle cross—for whom was it made?" And then He said, "Be careful before you answer."

I thought for a moment, then said, "It was made for Barabbas." He said, "That is right." I realized something that had never occurred to me before: the cross was there for Barabbas; it was waiting for him. But at the last moment, the Holy Spirit reminded me, Jesus took the place of Barabbas. "Yes," I affirmed.

Then it hit me. I was the criminal for whom the cross was made. It was fashioned to my measure. It stood where I deserved to hang. My old man deserved nothing less than the cross, but Jesus took my place. My old man was crucified in Him.

PRESSING AHEAD

I have not become perfect, but I am pressing upward toward the ultimate goal. I am not static or stuck in a rut. I am not a slave to traditions; I do not care what the world says or thinks. What matters to me is what God thinks. I have been delivered from slavery to the opinions of this world.

Paul said, in effect, "Through the cross, the world is crucified to me, and I am crucified to the world." (See Galatians 6:14.) In other words, Paul said that when the world looked at him, all they saw was a corpse hanging on a cross.

When Paul looked at the world, he saw the same thing—a corpse hanging on a cross. That was the value of the world to him; it held no

DO WE DESIRE RELEASE FROM
THE SLAVERY OF THE FLESH AND
THE WORLD? THERE IS ONE
WAY OUT: THE CROSS.

valuable charms. It did not impress him with its wealth, knowledge, or power, all of which are passing away. A new kingdom is coming—a kingdom that is not of this world. This kingdom is where I belong. It is the kingdom of my true, eternal citizenship.

Do we desire release from the slavery of the flesh and the world? There is one way out: the cross. Those who belong to Christ have crucified the flesh, along with its passions and desires. The world is crucified to me, and I to the world.

Thank God for the cross! If it were not for the cross, we would be slaves forever. The cross is our way to freedom. It is not a pain-free way, but *"he who has suffered in the flesh has ceased from sin"* (1 Peter 4:1). We can reach the point where we are so sick of our flesh that it can no longer tempt us to sin.

22

ENDURING TO THE END

In 2 Thessalonians 2, Paul wrote about the return of Jesus in power and glory to establish His kingdom on earth in place of the world's system:

> *Now, brethren, concerning the coming of our Lord Jesus Christ and our gathering together to Him, we ask you, not to be soon shaken in mind or troubled, either by spirit or by word or by letter, as if from us, as though the day of Christ had come.* (verses 1–2)

In other words, do not believe it when people tell you that the day of the Lord has come. People were already making this claim in Paul's day; some even circulated forged letters to this effect, pretending they were penned by Paul.

Paul continued his warning, *"Let no one deceive you by any means; for that Day will not come unless the falling away comes first, and the man of sin is revealed, the son of perdition"* (verse 3). The coming of the Lord will not happen until an apostasy; some to whom the truth has been revealed will reject it. Rejection necessitates initial reception, and where else can this occur but in the church, where the truth has been taught and received? In addition, the identity of the Antichrist will be known before the coming of the Lord. Keep this in mind.

THE TRUE CHURCH

In the *Battle of the Ages*, in which you and I are engaged, the true church is the great bulwark that protects the world from the Antichrist. But when the false church falls away from the true—when it succumbs to Satan's deception and breaks faithfulness to God—the bulwark will crumble, opening the way for the Antichrist to be revealed.

The false church's falling away factors into Satan's strategy to unveil the Antichrist. This is why we must learn to keep the two churches distinct and remain personally faithful to Christ.

Opposition will increase, but those who endure to the end will be saved. God will use the Antichrist's evil activities to refine the true church and bring forth a pure bride for the Lord Jesus Christ. Scripture declares that Christ's bride, the true church, will be glorious, holy, spotless, and without blemish. (See Ephesians 5:27.)

The Lord will lavish His love and blessing on His bride, the true church. Those who belong to the true church will share His throne throughout eternity. The false church, on the other hand, will be cast aside and rejected, a forgotten relic of history.

OPPOSITION WILL INCREASE,

BUT THOSE WHO ENDURE TO

THE END WILL BE SAVED.

OUR RELATIONSHIP WITH JESUS

Belonging to the true church is not a question of whether we prophesy or speak in tongues; it does not matter what particular mode of baptism we received or how many Scripture passages we have memorized. Rather, what matters is our personal relationship with Jesus Christ. Is He the Lord of our lives? Are we completely committed to Him? We prove our membership in the true church when we honor and serve the Lord, taking a stand for Him even in the face of opposition and persecution. We must put aside denominational labels and instead ask ourselves if we will we be faithful to Jesus.

We must resist the devil, repent of our sins, and submit to God, thereby thwarting Satan's dominion. If we love the truth, God will protect us from delusion.

A CLOSING PRAYER

If it is your desire to stay free of deception, and to be victorious in the *Battle of the Ages*, please pray this prayer with me now:

Heavenly Father, we come to You in the name of the Lord Jesus Christ, our wonderful Savior and our Lord. We thank You for the great salvation that You have purchased for us through the blood of Your Son. We do not take our salvation lightly. We thank You for the guidance You provide in the Scriptures, and we desire to live our lives according to what they teach us. We humble ourselves before You and acknowledge our total dependence upon You; it is only by Your faithfulness and mercy that we will be preserved.

Lord, we commit ourselves to You. We renounce any area in which deception may have gained some ground in our lives. We turn against it and drive it from us, loosening ourselves from its grasp in the name of Jesus.

We embrace the truth that is Jesus, the truth that is the Scriptures, and the truth that is the Holy Spirit. We open our hearts and minds to You, asking You to fill us with Your truth.

In Jesus's name, amen.

ABOUT THE AUTHOR

Derek Prince (1915–2003) was born in India of British parents. He was educated as a scholar of Greek and Latin at Eton College and King's College, Cambridge, in England. Upon graduation, he held a fellowship (equivalent to a professorship) in Ancient and Modern Philosophy at King's College. Prince also studied Hebrew, Aramaic, and modern languages at Cambridge and the Hebrew University in Jerusalem. As a student, he was a philosopher and a self-proclaimed agnostic.

While serving in the Royal Army Medical Corps (RAMC) during World War II, Prince began to study the Bible as a philosophical work. Converted through a powerful encounter with Jesus Christ, he was baptized in the Holy Spirit a few days later. Out of this encounter, he formed two conclusions: first, that Jesus Christ is alive; second, that the Bible is a true, relevant, up-to-date book. These conclusions altered the whole course of his life, which he then devoted to studying and teaching the Bible as the Word of God.

Discharged from the army in Jerusalem in 1945, he married Lydia Christensen, founder of a children's home there. Upon their marriage, he immediately became father to Lydia's eight adopted daughters—six Jewish, one Palestinian Arab, and one English. Together, the family saw the rebirth of the state of Israel in 1948. In the late 1950s, they adopted another daughter while Prince was serving as principal of a teachers' training college in Kenya.

In 1963, the Princes immigrated to the United States and pastored a church in Seattle. In 1973, Prince became one of the founders of Intercessors for America. His book *Shaping History Through Prayer and Fasting* has awakened Christians around the world to their responsibility to pray for their governments. Many consider underground translations of the book as instrumental in the fall of communist regimes in the USSR, East Germany, and Czechoslovakia.

Lydia Prince died in 1975, and Prince married Ruth Baker (a single mother to three adopted children) in 1978. He met his second wife, like his first wife, while she was serving the Lord in Jerusalem. Ruth died in December 1998 in Jerusalem, where they had lived since 1981.

Until a few years before his own death in 2003 at the age of eighty-eight, Prince persisted in the ministry God had called him to as he traveled the world, imparting God's revealed truth, praying for the sick and afflicted, and sharing his prophetic insights into world events in the light of Scripture. Internationally recognized as a Bible scholar and spiritual patriarch, Derek Prince established a teaching ministry that spanned six continents and more than sixty years. He is the author of more than eighty books, six hundred audio teachings, and one hundred video teachings, many of which have been translated and published in more than one hundred languages. He pioneered teaching on such groundbreaking themes as generational curses, the biblical significance of Israel, and demonology.

Prince's radio program, which began in 1979, has been translated into more than a dozen languages and continues to touch lives. Derek Prince's main gift of explaining the Bible and its teachings in a clear and simple way has helped build a foundation of faith in millions of lives. His nondenominational, nonsectarian approach has made his teaching equally relevant and helpful to people from all racial and religious backgrounds, and his messages are estimated to have reached more than half the globe.

In 2002, he said, "It is my desire—and I believe the Lord's desire—that this ministry continue the work, which God began through me over sixty years ago, until Jesus returns."

Derek Prince Ministries continues to reach out to believers in over 140 countries with Derek's teaching, fulfilling the mandate to keep on "until Jesus returns." This is accomplished through the outreaches of more than forty-five Derek Prince offices around the world, including primary work in Australia, Canada, China, France, Germany, the Netherlands, New Zealand, Norway, Russia, South Africa, Switzerland, the United Kingdom, and the United States. For current information about these and other worldwide locations, visit www.derekprince.org.

Welcome to Our House!

We Have a Special Gift for You

It is our privilege and pleasure to share in your love of Christian books. We are committed to bringing you authors and books that feed, challenge, and enrich your faith.

To show our appreciation, we invite you to sign up to receive a specially selected **Reader Appreciation Gift**, with our compliments. Just go to the Web address at the bottom of this page.

God bless you as you seek a deeper walk with Him!

WE HAVE A GIFT FOR YOU. VISIT:

whpub.me/nonfictionthx

WHITAKER
HOUSE

www.ingramcontent.com/pod-product-compliance
Lightning Source LLC
Chambersburg PA
CBHW051421090426
42737CB00014B/2765